Restless Devotion

*An Urgent Call
to Godward Discontentment*

Nick Thompson

Reformation Heritage Books
Grand Rapids, Michigan

Reformation Heritage Books
3070 29th St. SE
Grand Rapids, MI 49512
616-977-0889
orders@heritagebooks.org
www.heritagebooks.org

Printed in the United States of America
25 26 27 28 29 30/10 9 8 7 6 5 4 3 2 1

Library of Congress Cataloging-in-Publication Data

Names: Thompson, Nick (Theologian) author
Title: Restless devotion : an urgent call to Godward discontentment / Nick Thompson.
Description: Grand Rapids, Michigan : Reformation Heritage Books, [2025] | Summary: "An introductory study to show how the Psalms are intended to awaken Christians to a restless hunger for God"—Provided by publisher.
Identifiers: LCCN 2025004706 (print) | LCCN 2025004707 (ebook) | ISBN 9798886861822 paperback | ISBN 9798886861839 epub
Subjects: LCSH: Bible. Psalms—Criticism, interpretation, etc. | God—Biblical teaching | Christian life—Presbyterian authors
Classification: LCC BS1430.5 .T48 2025 (print) | LCC BS1430.5 (ebook) | DDC 223/.206—dc23/eng/20250326
LC record available at https://lccn.loc.gov/2025004706
LC ebook record available at https://lccn.loc.gov/2025004707

To Canon Elliot, Owen Ezra,
and Vos David

*May you far surpass your mother and me
in ravenous appetite for our gospel God*

Contents

The Vital Virtue of Discontentment

"Restlessness is discontent—and discontent is the first necessity of progress. Show me a thoroughly satisfied man—and I will show you a failure."

These are words the mastermind Thomas Edison recorded in his diary. Throughout his career Edison was awarded 1,093 US patents for his multiplicity of inventions. At his death he left behind over four thousand notebooks containing detailed records of his tireless drive for innovation.

As I write, an electric bulb hangs over my head, illuminating my desk. An electric bulb lies hidden behind the screen of my MacBook, illuminating my word processor. Thomas Edison did not invent the lightbulb, but he revolutionized it. In 1878 he filed a patent application for "improvement in electric lights." At this time electric bulbs had a short lifespan and were very expensive. Edison set out to change that, and through his invention of a carbon filament bulb that was both durable and economical, electric light became commonplace in America and around the world.

What drove Edison to labor for the improvement of electric bulbs? Discontentment. He was simply not satisfied with their low quality and high cost. That restless agitation of soul drove him to seek progress. Had he, along with the rest of humankind, been content with the bleak state of electric bulbs in the late nineteenth century, the average person would have no access to electric light today.

Discontent was arguably what fueled every one of Edison's ideas and inventions. His stubborn refusal to become "a thoroughly satisfied man" was what made him such a prolific success. In Edison's estimation, nothing was more detrimental than embracing the illusion that the human race had arrived. There was always more to discover, design, and develop. There was always progress to be made. His vision of better things to come provoked within him a restlessness that drove him to his dying day.

Discontent and Human Progress

Discontent is the necessary precondition of progress. If humans had been content with the outhouse and the bedpan, we wouldn't have indoor plumbing. If they had been content with the stagecoach, we wouldn't have automobiles and airplanes. If they had been content with sleepless nights in sweltering heat, we wouldn't have fans and air-conditioning units. Think of any of the modern-day innovations we enjoy. All of them were born out of discontent. In His common grace, God stirs up a productive restlessness in the hearts of men and women whom He gifts to make innovative progress in society. Without it, the human race may not have survived into the twenty-first century.

The book in your hands is about human progress, but not in the way Edison thought of it. I'm not seeking to promote progress in technology, medicine, econom-ics, education, or politics. While I'm deeply grateful for those making strides in these areas for the general good of humanity, these common-grace blessings have not actu-ally led to human progress in the ultimate sense. Given that humans are created in the image of God, true human progress is always progress toward God. And given the fall into sin, true human progress requires nothing less than God's saving grace transforming sinners in Jesus Christ. Tragically, however, humanity's innovative brilliance has often led society away from God and His saving grace and toward the idols of self-exaltation and self-salvation (see Gen. 11:1–9). Not everything that goes by the name of progress is true progress.

Restless Devotion encourages the promotion of prog-ress toward God in Christ. So why begin with Thomas Edison and lightbulbs? Though not a Christian, Edison is an exemplary illustration of the reality that progress results from dissatisfaction and rarely occurs without it. That is true when it comes to technological advances, but it is equally true when it comes to spiritual advances. To slightly modify Edison's assertion, "Show me a thoroughly satisfied Christian, and I will show you a spiritual failure." True spiritual progress is born out of holy discontentment.

Discontent and God

But wait a minute. Doesn't God call us to be content? Yes, He does: "Let your conduct be without covetousness; be content with such things as you have" (Heb. 13:5). Content-ment is not a divine suggestion; it is a divine imperative. We are to rest in God's providential plan for us, not enviously grasping after what He has not willed us to have (Psalm 131). In their exposition of the tenth commandment, "You shall not covet" (Ex. 20:17), the Westminster divines rightly teach us that God requires "full contentment with our own condition" and forbids "all discontentment with our own estate" (Westminster Shorter Catechism 80, 81). Contentment is the antithesis of covetousness. So, God commands us to be content, and furthermore, He reveals that contentment is the path to spiritual progress: "Now godliness with contentment is great gain. For we brought nothing into this world, and it is certain we can carry nothing out" (1 Tim. 6:6–7). Spiritual progress (i.e., "gain") is to be found in reflecting God (i.e., "godliness") and in resting in God (i.e., "contentment"). But doesn't this mean that spiritual success is obtained only by thoroughly satisfied Christians? It all depends on what you mean by *satisfied*.

God calls me, as a married man, to be content with the amazing wife He has blessed me with. To inordinately desire another man's wife is to fall into grave sin: "You shall not covet your neighbor's wife" (Ex. 20:17). I need to rest in God's all-wise providence and rejoice in His undeserved gift. In this sense the spiritual success of my marriage depends on me being thoroughly satisfied in my relationship with my wife, Tessa, before God. But after over a decade of marriage, our communication and selfless devotion toward one another is far from perfect. As a husband, I fail miserably at loving Tessa like Christ loves the church (Eph. 5:25). We haven't arrived as a couple, and I haven't arrived as a husband. There is tremendous progress to be made, and there ought to be a restless ache to make it. Without that ache, we will cease to grow as a married couple. In this sense, the spiritual success of my marriage depends on my being thoroughly dissatisfied in my relationship with Tessa before God. To be discontented with my marriage could be a vice, but it could also be a virtue.

That makes sense when you understand that discontentment is all about desire. You desire an object because you are dissatisfied without it. The Hebrew verb translated *covet* simply means "desire." In some contexts, it refers to godless desires, like the prohibition against covetousness in the tenth commandment (Ex. 20:17; Deut. 5:21). But in other contexts, it refers to godly desires, like when the psalmist extols God's word as "more to be *desired…* than gold, yea, than much fine gold" (Ps. 19:10; emphasis added). Christianity is not opposed to desire. God has wired us for desire. He has not merely given us an intellect to know and a will to choose, but He has also given us affections to desire. Holiness does not entail the suppression of desire; it entails the reformation of desire. Paul fleshes this out in Galatians 5:16–17: "But I say, walk by the Spirit, and you will not gratify *the desires* of the flesh. For *the desires* of the flesh are against the Spirit, and *the desires* of the Spirit are against the flesh, for these are opposed to each other" (ESV; emphasis added).

Discontentment, understood as a dissatisfied desire for an object we don't now possess, can be either a sinful vice or a spiritual virtue. What makes the difference? God does. The flesh produces a godless discontentment, whereas the Spirit produces a Godward discontentment.

Let's return to the marriage illustration. When a wife covets another woman's husband, she is harboring a dissatisfied desire that is anti-God. It is a desire that fails to be grateful to God and claims to know better than He does. It is a godless discontent, patterned after the inordinate desire that led to the downfall of the entire human race (see Gen. 3:6). But when that same wife is convicted over a pattern of sinful irritation and impatience toward her husband and it produces in her a dissatisfied desire to be more conformed to Christ in His gentleness and slowness to anger, this is a Godward discontentment. It is a desire that accords with God's will and aims at God's glory.

So, is it sinful to be discontented? It all depends on how your dissatisfied desire relates to God. God-suppressing desire is a vice, but God-serving desire is a virtue.

Discontent and Complacency

The burden of this book is that Godward desire is the necessary precondition of spiritual progress. Biblical spirituality pulsates with God-exalting dissatisfaction, and it perishes without it. That is why the call of *Restless Devotion* is urgent, for ordinarily, we make progress toward God only to the degree we desire it. If Edison had been content with candles and kerosene lanterns, he never would have developed a commercial incandescent bulb. If you and I are content with low levels of spirituality, we will never press on into the bright prospect of spiritual progress.

Spiritual complacency is one of our most dangerous foes and one of Satan's chief devices. Just as discontentment can be godless, so too can contentment. Complacency is a godless content, and one reason it is so dangerous is its subtlety. It can live and even thrive behind great religious externals. It infects Christians who hold fast to God-centered theology but smugly rest in their confessional orthodoxy as if it is an end in itself and not a means to an end of knowing God and reflecting Him. It infects churches that promote God-ordered worship but smugly rest in their adherence to the regulative principle without any concern whether the Spirit of God is actively working in their midst through the ordinary means of grace. It infects pastors and elders who shepherd the sheep entrusted to their care but smugly rest in the confines of their fold and never venture out in the uncomfortable pursuit of lost sheep. Spiritual complacency lulls us into a lackadaisical comatose state, and sadly, multitudes of Christians and churches succumb to Satan's soothing lullaby never to wake up again.

To be thoroughly satisfied in your present knowledge of God, likeness to God, and service to God equals the death of individual spiritual progress. To be thoroughly satisfied in your church's present worship, fellowship, and witness equals the death of corporate spiritual progress.

We must wake up! Those who are not progressing are digressing. It might be hard to see given the veneer of external religiosity that often continues unabated, but if we are not moving forward in experientially knowing and serving God, then we are most certainly moving backward. Our spirituality is never static. Unwarranted spiritual satisfaction always results in spiritual declension.

Discontent and the Already and Not Yet

Spiritual complacency is unwarranted for the simple reason that you and I have not arrived. As the church, we are living between the already of God's inaugurated kingdom and the not yet of God's consummated kingdom. As

Christians, we are living between the already of definitive deliverance from sin and the not yet of glorified deliverance from sin. God has brought us out of Egypt, but we have not yet reached the heavenly Canaan. We are in the wilderness, and the wilderness is no place to pitch our tents and get comfortable.

Think for a moment about your life before God. Do you treasure Him with all your heart, soul, mind, and strength? Is your prayer life everything it could be and should be? What about the motives that drive you to serve God and His people? Does your heart burn with a perfectly selfless, God-exalting, others-oriented affection? Are you seizing on the God-given moments, making the absolute best of every opportunity set before you? In your most intimate human relationships, do you flawlessly bear the fruit of "love, joy, peace, patience, kindness, goodness, faithfulness, gentleness, self-control" (Gal. 5:22–23 ESV)?

If you have the slightest measure of self-awareness, you responded with a matter-of-fact no to every one of those questions. I did the same. Why? Because we haven't arrived. Given the eschatological tension between the already and the not yet of our life in Christ, spiritual complacency is nothing less than spiritual madness. The same could be said with reference to the church and the world. This is no time for complacency!

Discontent and the Psalter

The book of Psalms gives us the clearest inspired window that we have into the inner workings of the Godward soul. These songs are written by wilderness people for wilderness people, and thus they are shot through with Godward discontentment. A restless longing pervades the Psalter, and without that restlessness we would not have it, for the psalmists' desperate pleas and delightful praises flow from hearts that are beautifully dissatisfied with the present state of affairs.

God gives us the Psalms to counter the satanic lullabies of complacency. But we need to do more than read and sing them if we are to be kept from drifting into spiritual sleep. We need to root the Psalms deep into our hearts so that they begin to form and reform our desires. We need the Holy Spirit to wield these inspired songs to awaken within us a restless hunger for God, His word, His salvation, His house, His restoration, His mission, and His vindication.

If God would see fit to use this little exposition of the Psalms to create and cultivate holy discontent in your heart, then I will rest content. Show me a Christian with a soul in the grip of Godward dissatisfaction, and I will show you a spiritual luminary.

CHAPTER 1

Restless for God

O God, You are my God;
Early will I seek You;
My soul thirsts for You;
My flesh longs for You
In a dry and thirsty land
Where there is no water.
—PSALM 63:1

Ichabod.

While Ham (Gen. 5:32), Mushi (Ex. 6:19), and Dodo (2 Sam. 23:24) compete for a close second, Ichabod is hands down the worst baby name ever given. To make matters worse, this poor boy's mother could barely get the name out of her mouth before she breathed her last. On the day of his birth, Ichabod lost his father, mother, grandfather, and uncle. It was a bleak beginning fitting for one endowed with such a bleak name. Ichabod means "no glory," and it referred to the glory of God. God's gracious manifestation of His weighty beauty was nowhere to be found in Israel.

Ichabod's grandfather Eli had been the high priest and judge of Israel in the days following Samson. It is hard to read the opening chapters of 1 Samuel without being struck between the eyes by Eli's spiritual complacency. His sons, serving as priests, had commercialized God's worship as a means to fill their bellies and had abused their authority as a means to gratify their lusts. Apart from giving them an insincere slap on the wrist, Eli was strangely indifferent toward the matter. While he ought to have been fasting in sackcloth, we find him feasting on sacrifices in a gluttonous slumber. Is it any wonder God was gone?

The externals of worship continued, but no one seemed to notice or care that God had not continued with His people—that was, until defeat at the hands of the Philistines resulted in the ark of the covenant being captured, leading to the agonizing cry of Eli's dying daughter, "Ichabod" (1 Sam. 4:21). God's glory was gone.

A Godward Bond

In every era, the chief treasure and boast of God's covenant people is the divine glory. The covenant is an exclusive communion bond wherein God gives Himself to His people as their exceeding great reward. From the human side, the covenant entails a threefold responsibility: seeing God's glory, savoring God's glory, and serving God's glory. But when Israel broke this exclusive union by uniting themselves to idols, God withdrew His gracious, soul-satisfying presence.

Ichabod is shorthand for covenant curse, and sadly, it is a summary of Israel's history. The God of glory gifted Himself to Israel as their supreme treasure, but they persistently refused to desire after and delight in Him. That refusal left a vacuum in their souls that they quickly filled with idols. This was what led to their undoing as a nation. This was what led to the ultimate curse of exile. Of the northern kingdom of Israel God said, "My people are destroyed for lack of knowledge" (Hos. 4:6). What kind of lacking knowledge was God indicting His people for? "There is no…knowledge of God in the land" (v. 1). Pervasive ignorance of God was the root problem in the northern kingdom, leading to their exile under Assyria. Sadly, the southern kingdom of Judah didn't learn from the Assyrian exile. They likewise hardened their hearts toward God's glorious self-revelation in the covenant:

> Can a virgin forget her ornaments,
> Or a bride her attire?
> Yet my people have forgotten Me days without
> number. (Jer. 2:32)

This was no innocent ignorance, for God exclaims, "Through deceit they refuse to know Me" (Jer. 9:6). A stubborn rejection of God's covenant glory was at the root of all the sinful folly of the southern kingdom and the great reason God exiled them under Babylon.

The covenant of grace is a relational bond in which God invites sinners into an intimate, experiential knowing of Himself through a mediator. But when the covenant people scorn that amazing invitation, it results in curse. Contrary to the thinking of many, the greatest threat to the late modern church is not expressive individualism, cultural Marxism, totalitarian statism, or moral relativism. Neither is it deficiency in prayer, evangelistic fervor, reverential worship, or holy living. These are all real threats in the visible church today that must be addressed and combated. But the root of all our unfaithfulness is always a sinful ignorance of the weighty God who gifts Himself to us in the covenant of grace. The root of all our sin is always idolatry, and idolatry is always at root a failure to relish intimate communion with our covenant Lord.

Only a few decades after the gloomy Ichabod ordeal, God's anointed king pours out his heart in wilderness prayer to his covenant Lord: "O God, You are my God" (Ps. 63:1). Take note of the personal pronoun *my*. David prays to the God who belongs to him. This is, after all, the essence of the covenant: "I will take you as My people, and I will be your God. Then you shall know that I am the LORD your God who brings you out from under the burdens of the Egyptians" (Ex. 6:7). David is bound to this God through His gracious condescension and deliverance, and it is on this basis that he prays. So it is with us. If we would pray like David does, we must know what it is to be delivered by God from our idolatry and restored to a loving communion bond with Him through the mediation of Jesus Christ.

A Godward Seeking

David is not enjoying a casual, fireside chat with God. He is desperate for his God, crying out, "O God, you are my God; earnestly I seek you" (Ps. 63:1 ESV). The language is strong. It could be translated as "desperately I seek You" or "wholeheartedly I seek You." This is a man in earnest who is in pursuit of a treasure he refuses to live without.

What is he seeking after? Given that he is on the run from his enemies in a barren wilderness (see the inscription to Psalm 63 and vv. 9–11), we might expect David to be seeking political power, physical provision, or military victory from God. As the anointed king of God's theocratic nation, it would have been entirely permissible for him to petition God for these things, but that is not what David does. David's wilderness plight drives him to seek not things from God, but God Himself: "earnestly I seek *you*" (v. 1; emphasis added).

Before it is anything else, prayer is covenantal communion with God. The heart of true prayer is not the pursuit of things from God but the pursuit of God Himself. Is that what drives your praying? Do you ever come before God not to seek things from Him but simply to seek Him? God invites us to seek things from Him, but there must be a Godward priority in all our praying that leads us to seek the Giver above His gifts.

The fascinating thing about David's cry is that in the same breath he speaks of having God and not having God. The God who is his through covenant and who is close enough to hear David's voice is the God whom David is chasing after through fervent prayer. David knows God and has God, but he is pursuing an expanding knowledge and possession of God. There is an already-not-yet dynamic to David's relationship with God, leading him to seek a closer walk and a renewed experience of the divine glory.

David can't fathom living in the land of Ichabod. He would rather die than succumb to an existence without the display of God's beauty through an expanding covenantal acquaintance. So, he cries out in whole-souled, ardent pursuit.

A Godward Desiring
It ought to be no surprise that this pursuit of progress toward God is the result of dissatisfied desire:

> My soul thirsts for You;
> My flesh longs for You
> In a dry and thirsty land
> Where there is no water. (Ps. 63:1)

As he journeyed through the waterless wilderness, David's brain sent neural signals to compel him to drink lest he die of dehydration. It's called *thirst*. Pondering this, David draws a parallel between his body's physical thirst and his soul's spiritual thirst. His soul is signaling a need to drink from the refreshing streams of God's life-giving glory. This spiritual thirst is so great that it is actually manifesting itself bodily (what he calls "my flesh"). The whole of David's redeemed humanity, body and soul, is craving God.

Do you remember Edison's words? "Restlessness is discontent—and discontent is the first necessity of progress." Millenia before Edison ever uttered or embodied these words, David did. The precondition of his spiritual progress toward God was a discontented desire for God. David is restless for God's covenantal glory.

Here is what we must grasp: You and I will never seek God earnestly until we long for Him intensely. If we are content with yesterday's encounter with God or last year's encounter with Him, we won't pursue an expanding acquaintance with God in the present. If we are satisfied with our current knowledge of God, we won't seek after deeper depths and higher heights. Earnest pursuit of God is always the result of holy dissatisfaction.

There is a rare disease called adipsia, which makes a person unable to thirst. It is a dangerous condition because a lack of thirst leads to a lack of water intake, and a lack of water intake leads to death. While adipsia is an uncommon physical condition, spiritual adipsia is not. It is a widespread disease that desensitizes the soul so that it no longer thirsts for the living waters of God's presence and grows content with going through the motions of religious exercises regardless of whether God is present or not. It turns prayer into a mere formality rather than a pursuit of soul-savoring fellowship with God.

Just as the healthy body sends nearly continuous signals for more water when in the wilderness, so too the healthy soul in this wilderness world is always sending signals for more of God. Imagine you are trudging through the Sahara with a friend, and you notice she is growing weaker and slower with every passing hour, so you ask, "Have you been drinking enough fluids?" She responds, "I don't need water. I drank plenty yesterday before we left on the journey." That is a great way to kill yourself! As it is with our bodies, so it is with our souls. We can't drink with the mouth of our souls on Sunday and expect it to sustain us the whole week. We can't be refreshed by God's glory on a weekend retreat and expect it to sustain us the whole year. Our souls are designed to drink continuously from God as He fills and satisfies us in His ever-unfolding fullness. Left unaddressed, spiritual adipsia could be the death of your soul.

So what is it that causes this antipathy toward God's glory? Why do we thirst for Him so little—or not at all? It is because, like Israel, we seek to quench our thirst with the idols of our making:

> For My people have committed two evils:
> They have forsaken Me,
> > the fountain of living waters,

And hewn themselves cisterns—
    broken cisterns that can hold no water.
    (Jer. 2:13)

The reason we don't thirst for God as we ought is because we drink from earthly alternatives, seeking ultimate soul satisfaction in entertainment, money, sex, romance, beauty, physical health, or human achievement and accolades.

If you sense in your soul a deficiency of Godward craving, the reason is very simple. Spiritual adipsia is always the result of spiritual idolatry. Treasuring the things of the creation (even good things) above the Creator deceives us into thinking we are satisfied when, in fact, we are starving.

One of the great gifts of the wilderness is that it strips us of the created things our idolatrous hearts are prone to worship. David cannot look to power, popularity, or prosperity to satisfy him while he is a desert fugitive on the run. God tailor-makes our trials and tribulations to strip us of our idols so that our souls may learn to thirst for Him, for it is only such restless desire that will drive us to ardent pursuit. Have you considered that the trials you are undergoing may be God's way of delivering you from your sinful substitutes for His all-satisfying glory?

A Godward Knowing

David's restless desire for God, which is leading him to earnestly pursue God, is rooted in his past experience of God. He recounts,

So I have looked upon you in the sanctuary,
beholding your power and glory.

> Because your steadfast love is better than life,
> my lips will praise you. (Ps. 63:2–3 ESV)

He recalls a time when his heart had gazed on God's manifest beauty in the midst of the tabernacle. To mix metaphors, David had drunk with his eyes. His soul had seen and savored a breathtaking panorama of divine glory, and, having drunk deeply, he is now longing for more. Having been the recipient of this incredible self-disclosure of God, he desires a fresh sight of Him whose covenant affection is more precious than life itself.

Since God's glory is boundless, the more we come to know Him, the more we recognize how little we know Him. As we revel in the revealed mystery of God's being, our inability to comprehend Him fully leaves a restless ache to plunge deeper into the mystery of who He is. There is always more to discover and delight in.

After ten years of marriage to Tessa, I know her far better than I did on our wedding day. Yet she is more of a mystery to me today than she was when I said, "I do." If you were to seriously ask me, "Nick, do you think you will ever comprehend Tessa?" your question will be met with a belly laugh. "Comprehend her? Are you kidding?" Now you might think that the inability to exhaustively know her would lead to indifference in my pursuit of her. After all, what's the point of trying? But in actual experience, it has the opposite effect. The more I come to know and enjoy her within this covenant bond, the more I long to know and enjoy her better. If that is true of a finite creature, how much more so the infinite Creator!

David's past covenantal communion with God is driving him with desperate desire to have more of God. This is what the godly soul does. It strains all its limited, creaturely faculties to apprehend as much of the limitless glory of God that it possibly can. Having seen God's beauty, the soul longs to see more. Having drunk of God's glory, the soul longs to drink deeper still.

In reading of David's intense desire for God, if you find yourself thinking he is over the top with religious fanaticism, it may be because your soul has never tasted or seen the goodness of the Lord, for David is exemplifying nothing more than a healthy wilderness spirituality. If it seems extreme to you, it may be because you don't know God. Have you drunk of Him? Have you seen Him? Have you been born again? The pursuit of God begins with a saving sight of God in the gospel that leaves us longing for more.

So there is a certain order to biblical spirituality that David models for us. Knowing God leads the soul to desire God, and desiring God leads the soul to seek God. To such a soul, God delights in manifesting His glory.

A Godward Finding

In absolute confidence that his passionate pursuit of God will not leave him empty, David declares,

> My soul shall be satisfied as with marrow
>   and fatness,
> And my mouth shall praise You with joyful lips.
> When I remember You on my bed,
> I meditate on You in the night watches.
>   (Ps. 63:5–6)

David is confident that as he seeks God, remembering Him even through the watches of the night, his soul will be stuffed with the riches of divine glory. There is a soul feast on David's horizon that will result in soul satisfaction, and he refuses to let God go until he experiences it: "My soul clings to you" (Ps. 63:8 ESV).

In our pursuit of God, He is often slow to disclose more of Himself to us. He rarely responds to our seeking with immediate gratification. Why? Because the deeper the thirst is, the deeper the delight in drinking will be. The more intense the hunger pangs are, the more ravenous the feasting will be. It is through the watches of the night while complacent souls sleep that patient perseverance is cultivated through a refusal to let God go until He blesses us with Himself.

As David clutches God with the hands of his soul, God is clutching David with His anthropomorphic hand: "My soul clings to you; your right hand upholds me" (Ps. 63:8 ESV). We could call it the double-clutch of deep communion. The godly grasp tightly to God even as they are grasped tightly by God. The verb translated "clings" in verse 8 is the same one used in God's institution of the covenant of marriage: "Therefore a man shall leave his father and mother and *be joined* [i.e., "cling"] to his wife, and they shall become one flesh" (Gen. 2:24; emphasis added). This is an intimate, loving grip of exclusive devotion, and just as in the covenant of marriage, both parties hold fast to one another in the covenant of grace.

Throughout David's entire prayer, God has been upholding David. God brought to remembrance the past experience of His glory. God sent the spiritual signals of hunger and thirst for a deeper experience of His glory. God strengthened David's soul as he pursued His glory.

This is all of grace! And given that God has brought all this about, David is confident that though God may tarry, He will not fail to satisfy his soul afresh and anew. His pursuit of God will result in progress in his seeing, savoring, and serving God.

As we seek after God in Christ, according to His word and in dependence on His Spirit, we can take heart that those who seek Him find Him. You and I have as much of God as we want. If we know Him little, it is because we want Him little. But the soul that is large with Godward appetite is a soul that is progressively fattened with God's delicious glory.

Do you see how Godward discontent is the first necessity of progress toward God?

The *Ordo Devotionis*

In theology we speak of the *ordo salutis*, a Latin term that means "order of salvation." It refers to the logical order of the benefits of salvation in Christ. Psalm 63 reveals what we could call the *ordo devotionis*, or "order of devotion." This is the order in which our devotion to God is cultivated and expressed within the covenant of grace. It consists of four basic components: knowing God, desiring God, seeking God, finding God.

But this order does not play itself out in a straight line. It unfolds in an ever-expanding circle. God draws us into the knowledge of Himself, which then causes us to desire more of Him. That desire for God causes us to seek after Him. That seeking after Him results in us finding Him. And here is the beautiful reality: The deeper experiential knowledge of God that we obtain in finding Him makes us desire more, which causes us to seek more, which causes us to find more. Here is what it looks like:

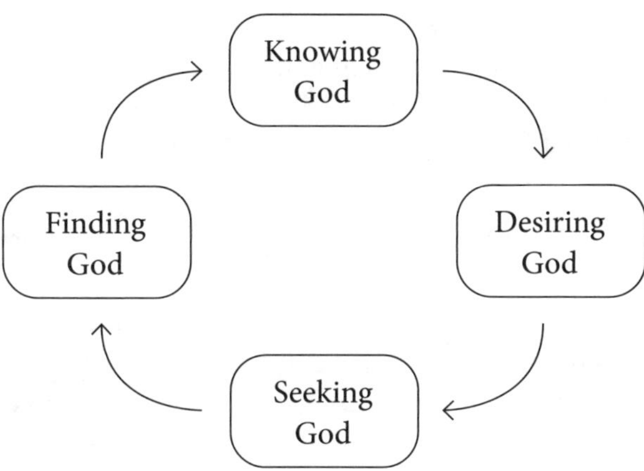

The healthy soul never graduates from the *ordo devotionis* while journeying through the wilderness of this world, for there is always more of God to discover and delight in. It is spiritual complacency that keeps our souls from orbiting the circle of Godward devotion, molding us into spiritual failures like Eli who rest content with *Ichabod* written on the doorposts of our hearts. God forbid that such would be true of us!

We must take care not to go the way of the northern kingdom of Israel but instead heed God's call:

> Let us know; let us press on to know the LORD;
> his going out is sure as the dawn;
> he will come to us as the showers,
> as the spring rains that water the earth.
> (Hos. 6:3 ESV)

We must take care not to go the way of the southern kingdom of Judah but instead heed God's call:

> Let not the wise man glory in his wisdom,
> Let not the mighty man glory in his might,
> Nor let the rich man glory in his riches;
> But let him who glories glory in this,
> That he understands and knows Me.
> (Jer. 9:23–24)

God delights in those who make an expanding and experiential knowledge of Him their chief pursuit and chief praise. This is the path to keeping covenant, and it is the very reason why the new covenant will not end in exile. Through Christ's death and resurrection, God is reconciling sinners like us to Himself, radically renovating their souls and delivering them from their idols so that God can say of them, "No more shall every man teach his neighbor, and every man his brother, saying, 'Know the LORD,' for they all shall know Me, from the least of them to the greatest of them" (Jer. 31:34). Christ endured the exile that our covenant-breaking idolatry deserves so that we can know covenant blessing, which is nothing less than knowing the covenant God Himself: "And this is eternal life, that they may know You, the only true God, and Jesus Christ whom You have sent" (John 17:3).

The gospel beckons God's wilderness people into an expanding, intimate, covenantal knowing of Him. Show me the soul that craves after that, and I will show you a man or woman who is the object of God's eternal delight. Show me the soul who restlessly aches for God, and I will show you a spiritual success in Christ.

CHAPTER 2

Restless for God's Word

I opened my mouth and panted,
For I longed for Your commandments.
—PSALM 119:131

Lying open on the table next to me is a leather-bound copy of the Bible in the English language. It cost me roughly seventy dollars, but what I can so easily forget is that it cost men like William Tyndale their lifeblood.

It is hard to imagine, but there was a day when the English-speaking world did not have access to the Scriptures in the common language. The Roman Catholic Church, with the sanction of the civil magistrate, forbid printing, reading, and teaching the Bible in English. Those caught doing so were burned at the stake. This was a powerplay on the part of Rome, for the pope and his priests understood that if the Bible got into the heads and hearts of the common people, the church's man-made doctrines and practices would be exposed.

In stepped William Tyndale, a Roman Catholic priest and an incredibly gifted linguist. Through Luther's books and Erasmus's Greek New Testament, his eyes had been opened to the doctrine of justification by faith alone while a student at Cambridge. Tyndale was transformed by God's word, causing him to burn with an all-consuming passion to publish that word for the world. He devoted his life to this cause, producing the first English translation of the Bible from the original Greek and Hebrew.

This, of course, was illegal. Tyndale sought permission from the bishop of London in 1524, but it was not granted. So for the next decade, he lived in Germany and the Netherlands as a hunted fugitive, undergoing great hardship as he gave himself to the arduous work of Bible translation. When King Henry VIII appealed to him to come back to England, Tyndale agreed to return and die whatever death the king deemed appropriate as long as Henry would agree to legalize the distribution of the English New Testament. But Henry refused.

Tyndale's New Testament translation was smuggled into England and Scotland, and it spread like wildfire. Tragically, it resulted in fire of another kind, for those found in possession of it were burned alive. James Bainham was one of many who lost his life. In the middle of a Mass in 1532, he stood up in St. Augustine's Church, raised high a copy of Tyndale's New Testament, and pled with those present to die rather than deny the Word of God. Die he did.

Tyndale understood that those caught with copies of his translation would be martyred. But he couldn't stop, and he wouldn't stop until he himself was betrayed, arrested, and imprisoned. After eighteen months of intense suffering and attempted brainwashing, Tyndale was tied to the stake on October 6, 1536. As he was strangled with a metal chain, he cried out, "Lord! Open the king of

England's eyes!" His body was then set ablaze, followed by sprinkling gunpowder on his ashes as his remains were blown to smithereens.

Tyndale never married. He was never buried. He was publicly executed in the most horrific way. Why? Because of the Bible.

A Covenantal Word Worth Dying For

Tyndale understood that for sinners like us to come to a saving knowledge of God, we need a saving revelation from God. For the covenant God to be known and enjoyed, His covenant word is absolutely necessary. Throughout every epoch of covenant history, God has revealed Himself through human words, accommodating His unspeakable glory to our creaturely vernacular. Tyndale and so many others spilled their blood for us to have the Bible in our tongue because they understood that through this book the objective shafts of God's soul-satisfying beauty shine, and without this book humanity is in the dark.

It is just this conviction that gave rise to the opening words of the Psalter. Psalm 1, functioning as an introduction to the entire book of Psalms, sets before us the path of blessedness. Everyone on the planet wants to be blessed, but there are two conflicting sources of authority defining blessedness and delineating how to obtain it: the depraved world and the divine word.

In our fallen nature, we choose the first, walking in "the counsel of the ungodly," standing "in the path of sinners," and sitting "in the seat of the scornful" (Ps. 1:1). In Adam we embrace the world's definition of blessedness.

What is that definition? You don't need to look any further than the magazine racks in your local supermarket:

- *Prevention* tells us that blessedness is found in the body. The root of happiness is physical health and appearance.

- *Forbes* tells us that blessedness is found in the bank. The root of happiness is material wealth.

- *Cosmopolitan* tells us that blessedness is found in the bedroom. The root of happiness is the ultimate sexual experience.

- *Parents* magazine tells us that blessedness is found in the bloodline. The root of happiness is children who are successful and productive members of society.

I could give even more examples. But it is not necessary, for they all are symptomatic of the same deadly disease—idolatry. Their message is that ultimate satisfaction is found in created things rather than in the Creator. Apart from God's saving revelation, this is the company we keep and the worldview we embrace. This pursuit leads not to the blessedness it promises, but to curse.

True blessedness is found in whole-souled devotion to "the law [Hebrew, Torah] of the LORD" (Ps. 1:2). *Torah* is an elastic term that often, especially in wisdom literature, refers more broadly to teaching. This is the instruction that comes from God's mouth, and it is instruction that is always covenantal (hence, God's covenant name, Yahweh). Through this word, sinners are led to abandon the world's folly, being born again into a gracious, covenantal bond with God, the sum and substance of true blessedness. God's covenant people are willing to die, if necessary, to preserve and propagate the Scriptures because without them their blessed God cannot be known and enjoyed.

Aching with Desire for the Word

From the start of our relationship, Tessa and I have written paper-and-ink love letters to each other. To this day, Tessa's letters have the ability to melt my heart. But they have never been more precious to me than during a period of our engagement when we were geographically separated from each other. Unable to communicate by telephone because of Tessa's deafness, we relied entirely on written words. The physical separation morphed my longing for her into a longing for her letters. I had never been so eager for the mailman to arrive, restless with desire for a fresh communication from her pen.

In the time between the already of God's inaugurated kingdom and the not yet of God's consummated kingdom, there is a very real sense in which we have a long-distance relationship with God. That is not to downplay the dynamic indwelling of the Holy Spirit in our hearts or our vital union with the Christ of heaven. But it is to say that we are not yet with God in glory. We are in the wilderness. So, too, is the psalmist. The writer of the longest song in the Psalter, devoted to extolling God's Torah, refers to himself as "a stranger in the earth" (Ps. 119:19). He is a pilgrim like us, and his wilderness trials and temptations are driving him to God's covenant word with restless desire. His soul gives vent to this Godward discontent, exclaiming, "I opened my mouth and panted, for I longed for Your commandments" (v. 131). This is no flash-in-the-pan desire, but the steady state of his innermost being.

"My soul breaks with longing for Your judgments at all times" (v. 20).

For many of us, the psalmist's claim is so foreign that we automatically assume he must be exaggerating. It just seems a bit over the top. The Bible is great and all, but this man almost sounds like he has lost his mind!

Consider, however, that if exaggeration is a form of lying, and lying is a violation of the ninth commandment, then we cannot conclude that this man, under the inspiration of the Holy Spirit, catered to such sinful embellishment.

Has he lost his mind? No more than the twitterpated fiancée checking her mailbox every hour for a letter from her man. The lover, separated from her beloved, craves written communication from him.

Our wilderness separation from God is temporary. There will come a time when we won't need the sixty-six love letters He has written us in the Old and New Testaments. A time is coming when our long-distance engagement to Christ (what the Bible calls *betrothal*) will give way to consummate marriage. On that day we won't have our faces glued to a book, even the Book of books. What a sorry state of affairs it would be if, as Tessa walked down the aisle on our wedding day radiant with beauty, I stood at the altar with my face buried in her love letters and failed to even notice her! When we get to glory, beholding Him face-to-face, we won't need the Bible anymore. But the distance between us now, as our Lord is in heaven and we are on earth, makes His written words supremely desirable. For without them, we don't have Him.

In the wilderness, the soul's restless ache for more of God translates into a restless ache for more of His word.

Aching with Delight in the Word

Let's return to my engagement to Tessa. The mailman has just arrived, and I am excitedly running down the stairs and out the door like a little boy on Christmas morning. I open the mailbox and quickly start flipping through the envelopes. There might be a birthday card from Grandma with cash in it. There might be an advertisement from my favorite store. But the moment I spot Tessa's handwriting, every other piece of mail is dismissed as junk (sorry, Grandma!). My treasuring Tessa translates into a treasuring of her words.

This is like the blessed man, who doesn't just have the word of God but "*delights*" in it (Ps. 1:2; emphasis added). Notice the words of the sojourner in Psalm 119:

- "I have rejoiced in the way of Your testimonies, as much as in all riches" (v. 14).

- "Your testimonies are my delight" (v. 24).

- "I will delight myself in Your commandments, which I love" (v. 47).

- "The law of Your mouth is better to me than thousands of coins of gold and silver" (v. 72).

- "I have seen the consummation of all perfection, but Your commandment is exceedingly broad" (v. 96).

- "Oh, how I love Your law!" (v. 97).

- "How sweet are Your words to my taste, sweeter than honey to my mouth!" (v. 103).

- "Your testimonies I have taken as a heritage forever, for they are the rejoicing of my heart" (v. 111).

- "I love Your commandments more than gold, yes, than fine gold!" (v. 127).

- "Your word is very pure; therefore Your servant loves it" (v. 140).

- "I rejoice at Your word as one who finds great treasure" (v. 162).

- "My soul keeps Your testimonies, and I love them exceedingly" (v. 167).

This man has a love affair with the word of God! This raises an important question: What makes this any different from the idolatry of the wicked? After all, the Bible is a paper-and-ink book. It is a part of creation, is it not? Has this man fallen prey to bibliolatry?

Bibliolatry can certainly happen, but it is most certainly not what is happening here. The reason his heart is thrilling in God's self-revelation with an aching affection and all-consuming delight is because his heart thrills in God Himself. He treasures the book of God because He treasures God.

If a choice had to be made between a prosperous life of ease ("thousands of gold and silver pieces") without the Scriptures or an impoverished life of suffering with the Scriptures, the decision is a no-brainer for the psalmist. "Take the godless world, but give me God's word!"

Given who God is, the seventy-dollar, beat-up Bible beside me is infinitely more valuable than the net worth of Jeff Bezos, Elon Musk, and Bill Gates combined. Let that sink in for a moment. Do you treasure the Bible like that? Do you ache with desire for the Word of God? This is the path of progress toward God. For such discontent drives us to grapple with God's word in an ever-deepening way.

Aching to Digest the Word

The Bible calls such inward grappling *meditation*. The blessed man's delight in God's Torah is the grand reason why "he meditates day and night" on it (Ps. 1:2). The cry of the Godward soul is, "Oh, how I love Your law! It is my meditation all the day" (119:97).

Meditation refers to deep, prolonged reflection in the mind and heart. It mulls over its object perpetually in the pursuit of seeing the fullness of what is really there. For example, take *blessed*, which is the first word of both Psalm 1 and Psalm 119. Spend three hours chewing on that. Turn it over in your mind. Ponder it in your heart. Preach it to yourself. Question it:

- Why would God begin the Psalter with this word?

- Is there a person alive who doesn't want to be blessed? Why is that? What explains the innate human propensity toward blessedness?

- Is the psalmist intentionally playing on that universal desire to get our attention?

- What does *blessed* mean? Is it an emotional capacity? Is it an outward condition? Is it a combination of both?

- Who determines what is blessed and what is not?

- How does the blessedness in Psalm 1 relate to the blessedness of Psalm 119?

- Are there other places in Scripture where this term

is used that might shed light on its meaning in
these texts?

- How do I know if I am blessed?

- How is it even possible for a sinner who deserves
God's curse to be blessed?

- Am I blessed?

Suddenly a word that you thought you understood shows itself to have a depth and profundity that warrants hours of pondering.

Meditation is an exceedingly thorough grappling with the word of God that literally has no end. Our finite minds and hearts will never come close to reaching the infinite depths of divine glory revealed in the word. That is the reason for "day and night" (Ps. 1:2) and "all the day" (119:97). This man is not content with his present grasp of God through the word. He wants more! He is not checking off his Bible reading for the day in order to appease his conscience and get on with it. He has come to the word in restless pursuit of a deeper experiential knowledge of the one his soul loves.

In the months before our wedding, I would read Tessa's love letters over and over, savoring every word. Almost always, her letters would begin with the three words "My Dearest Nicholas." I would mull over them with hungry delight: *"My." She is saying I am hers! If that is not enough, she modified my name with the superlative "dearest." That means there is no man dearer to her than I am! And she called me by my full name, which for some reason doesn't bother me like it does when Mom calls me Nicholas. Instead, it is strangely endearing and romantic.* Slowly, I would work my way through her letter, unpacking every word and phrase, and when I finished I would do it all over again.

The blessed man has a love affair with the word of God because he has a love affair with God Himself, and so he is continuously meditating. He is seeking to digest God's word as the path of satisfying His restless soul with God. But because he understands that this kind of spiritual digestion is ultimately God's work, he prays to God even as he chews on God's word:

- "Teach me Your statutes" (Ps. 119:12).

- "Open my eyes, that I may see wondrous things from Your law" (v. 18).

- "Do not hide Your commandments from me" (v. 19).

- "Make me understand the way of Your precepts" (v. 27).

- "Strengthen me according to Your word" (v. 28).

There is a restless ache to know and understand the Word of God and a humble realization that only God can grant it. You can get a PhD in the Bible and be entirely ignorant of God. It requires the Holy Spirit's gracious work of illumination to draw us into a true knowledge of God through the word He inspired.

Do you pray in desperation for deeper understanding when you come to your Bible in private worship, family worship, and public worship? Or are you complacently satisfied with the stale insights of days gone by?

Show me the Christian who is thoroughly satisfied with their knowledge of the Scriptures, and I will show you a spiritual failure.

Aching to Do the Word

It is easy to think that by *knowledge of the Scriptures*, I simply mean intellectual understanding. I do mean that, but I don't simply mean that. For true knowledge gained through Spirit-blessed meditation doesn't just overtake the head, but also the heart and hands. This sojourner is restless not merely to get his theology figured out but for his life to conform perfectly to the word of God. "Oh, that my ways were directed to keep Your statutes!" (Ps. 119:5). This is why he cries out for illumination as He meditates: "I will run in the way of your commandments when you enlarge my heart" (v. 32 ESV).

Does your heart feel narrow? Mine does, and try as I might, I can't do anything to change it. Only God can cause this sinful heart to swell with enlarging love for Him and His image-bearing creatures. The chief instrument God uses to expand our affections so that our feet joyously run on the narrow path of holiness is the Bible.

Those who are content to hear and understand the Bible without bringing their desires, words, and actions into alignment with the Bible are in a woeful condition. What happens to the woman's heart when she reads the letter from her beloved who is off in a distant land? Those words cause her heart to expand with love toward him, and that expanding love evidences itself in an expanding desire to please him. This is why a Spirit-wrought appetite for the Scriptures will always result in a Spirit-wrought appetite for holiness. It can't be otherwise for the soul who aches with longing for God's glorious self-disclosure in the word.

The psalmist's restless desire for conformity to God's word is not an individualistic desire. Yes, he longs for holiness in his life. But as he looks at the godless world around him that has rejected God's word, his soul cries in discontented lament, "Rivers of water run down from my eyes, because men do not keep Your law" (Ps. 119:136). He is hungry for every image-bearing creature to reflect the Creator in knowledge, righteousness, and holiness, and the hunger is engrossing: "My zeal has consumed me, because my enemies have forgotten Your words" (v. 139). This man has tasted and seen the goodness of God in the word, and he longs for others to do the same.

A Covenantal Word We Idolatrously Reject

The man behind Psalm 119 may be a spiritual giant, but the reality is that he does not perfectly delight in, desire, digest, or do God's word. That is why he ends with a confession: "I have gone astray like a lost sheep; seek Your servant" (v. 176). This should be an encouragement to us in our weakness. We need God, as our Good Shepherd, to seek us out and rescue us from our sheepish folly. With a deep sense of his proneness to wander from God and His word, the psalmist petitions,

> Incline my heart to Your testimonies,
> And not to covetousness.
> Turn away my eyes from looking at worthless
>   things,
> And revive me in Your way. (Ps. 119:36–37)

Our hearts naturally pursue selfish gain and worthless things to the neglect of the Scriptures. Worldlings give themselves to the restless pursuit of selfish gain, living for money, possessions, popularity, promotions, and power.

They hungrily fix their eyes on worthless things, endlessly scrolling their social media feeds, binge-watching Netflix, and feeding on sexually explicit images. Like the psalmist, we need to realize that is where our hearts will go if God doesn't supernaturally intervene. In our folly we exchange God's worthy word for worthless things. No one except God Himself can deliver us from it!

Do you find a lack of desire in your heart toward the Scriptures? Repentance is what is needed, and if your heart is anything like mine, repentance is continually needed. Turn from your worldly, godless folly to God in and through Christ. It is Christ, God's final Word, who alone perfectly desired, delighted in, digested, and did God's word. He came into the world declaring,

> Behold, I come;
> In the scroll of the book it is written of me.
> I delight to do Your will, O my God,
> And Your law is within my heart. (Ps. 40:7–8)

Christ possessed such an agitated desire for the worldly wicked to be brought into the blessedness of communion with God through His word that He bled and died in agonizing torment. Is your heart cold to the word of God? Then turn from your idols to God through Him and plead with God, "Incline my heart to Your testimonies!" A repentant and believing prayer like that cannot go unanswered.

A Covenantal Word That Sustains

During a long-distance engagement, written communication is key to maintaining and deepening the relationship. There is a sense in which those letters between Tessa and me sustained us through the weary and difficult days we were apart. Had I ignored her communication to me and failed to respond, we would not be married today.

The professing Christian who is indifferent toward God's communication and fails to respond in prayer and praise will not make it to the divine-human wedding on the horizon. The psalmist confesses that apart from his desire-filled pleasure in God's word, he would have died in the wilderness: "Unless Your law had been my delight, I would then have perished in my affliction" (Ps. 119:92). This delightful word from our loving God is what sustains the souls of pilgrims through the tribulations we face here below.

This is why a man like Tyndale would spill his blood to propagate the Scriptures. As Tyndale was strangled and set ablaze, he heralded Psalm 119:161–62:

> Princes persecute me without a cause,
> But my heart stands in awe of Your word.
> I rejoice at Your word
> As one finds great treasure.

God's word sustained him to the end, and through his sacrifice we now have the awesome privilege of possessing it and possessing God through it.

If we are to be a people who thrive by God's covenantal grace, we must thrill in His covenantal word. If we are to know true blessedness, we must burn with restless desire for an expanding and transforming knowledge of God through the Spirit-illuminated Scripture. This is the path to spiritual progress.

CHAPTER 3

Restless for God's Salvation

Make me hear joy and gladness,
That the bones You have broken may rejoice.
Hide Your face from my sins,
And blot out all my iniquities.
—PSALM 51:8–9

In the summer of 2018, twelve boys and their soccer coach journeyed miles into the Tham Luang cave in northern Thailand. What began as an afternoon of innocent fun quickly turned into a deadly ordeal as heavy rainfall flooded the cave, trapping the thirteen people deep inside. A week passed without any sign of the floodwaters receding as these boys sat in darkness with little food, deficient oxygen, and absolutely no way of escape. Given that it was monsoon season, the likelihood of the cave being entirely submerged beneath water was great, and the two-and-a-half-mile dive out, with its strong currents and narrow passageways, was simply impossible for them to swim.

If you had the ability to read the hearts of those thirteen people in their helpless misery, do you know what you would have found? A restless ache for rescue. That is why when two British divers discovered them on the eighth day of their captivity, their tired, malnourished, confused faces couldn't help but smile. It would take another ten days for these divers and their team to get the boys out, and because of the grave dangers associated with doing so, it was necessary for them to use anesthetics to put the soccer team members to sleep as they carried them through the deadly floodwaters to safety.

It is a striking picture of us in the darkness of our native depravity and sinful inability. When we come to grasp our desperate condition in Adam by the Holy Spirit's convicting power, it provokes within us an ache for spiritual rescue.

By the time David writes Psalm 51, he is a believer who knows what it is to be rescued by God from the condemnation and corruption of his sin. Through the gospel, David's heart has been recreated after God's heart. But he is still a sinner who is capable of the most grotesque forms of rebellion imaginable, which is why the inscription to Psalm 51 reads, "A Psalm of David, when Nathan the prophet went to him, after he had gone in to Bathsheba." David, the recipient of God's unspeakable goodness, willfully ran into the path of unspeakable badness. Driven by a heart of lust, he slept with another man's wife, deceiving and murdering to cover it up (2 Sam. 11:2–27).

What gave rise to this shocking scandal? Complacency. At "the time when kings go out to battle" to conquer and extend the borders of their kingdoms, "David remained at Jerusalem" in leisurely ease (2 Sam. 11:1). God's man fell prey to a smugness that led to his downfall, and the scariest thing about it was his stubborn refusal to seek the only One who could rescue him. David successfully silenced his conscience and hid his shameful actions from the eyes of others, and he had every intention of moving on as if nothing had happened. But he could not hide his sin from the eyes of God, nor could he silence the piercing rebuke of God's prophet, "You are the man!" (2 Sam. 12:7). God, in His gospel goodness, came after David, laying him bare in his sin so that he would hunger and thirst after divine rescue.

Desperate Conviction of Sin

Not all conviction of sin is godly (2 Cor. 7:10). The tell-tale sign of a carnal conviction of sin is that it drives the soul away from God instead of toward Him. David's conscience had sounded the alarm in the aftermath of his sin. But that conviction led him to concoct a godless plan to cover it up. It wasn't until the word of God through Nathan cut David deep that he experienced a Godward conviction, provoking him to plead,

> Have mercy upon me, O God,
> According to Your lovingkindness;
> According to the multitude of Your tender mercies,
> Blot out my transgressions. (Ps. 51:1)

David is restless for God to freshly display mercy toward him. Divine mercy is the tender pity God exercises toward sinners and sufferers in their misery. David's sin left him in a miserable condition, but he appeals to the God who is compassionate toward the miserable, especially when they are His own covenant people. He pleads for God to show mercy "according to [His] lovingkindness," a reference to the covenantal affection by which He treasures His people. Furthermore, though he doesn't use the term here, David seeks God's grace, the free favor He shows to those who deserve just the opposite. I can say that because David doesn't deserve to be the recipient of God's mercy or His love, which is a gracious mercy and a gracious love. The realization of David's sin is driving Him to seek the God who in mercy tenderly pities, in love affectionately treasures, and in grace freely favors. David is aching for a renewed experience of God's gospel goodness, and that ache is causing him to pursue it with desperate intensity.

Between the already of our definitive deliverance from sin and the not yet of our consummate deliverance from sin, this is our prayer. Psalm 51 is not reserved for only "big" sins. It is the healthy cry of the believer in the aftermath of any and every sin, and it begins with turning to the God of large-hearted gospel goodness. This is always God's purpose in bringing conviction to us. He convinces us of our misery in order that we, like the prodigal, will return to our Father in the restless pursuit of mercy (Luke 15:17).

Desperate Confession of Sin

The genuine conviction of sin that drives us to God drives us to Him in confession. The sin that God has brought before David, David now brings before God:

> For I acknowledge my transgressions,
> And my sin is always before me.
> Against You, You only, have I sinned,
> And done this evil in Your sight—
> That You may be found just when You speak,
> And blameless when you judge. (Ps. 51:3–4)

True confession of sin condemns the self and justifies the Lord.

If we were unaware of the historical context, we would likely conclude that the sin being confessed here is between David and God alone. But David sinned against Bathsheba, luring her into his bedroom. He sinned against Uriah, robbing him of his wife and his life. He sinned against his family and his nation, who will suffer immensely for his infidelity. Yet as David comes before God, he doesn't say a word about any of that, at least not directly. He is consumed with the reality that his sin is against God: "Against You, You only, have I sinned." The only One who can rescue David is the One whom David has rebelled against.

Before our sin is against our fellow creatures, it is first and foremost against our Creator, who in Christ has become our Redeemer. Our sin is anti-God. That is what makes every sinful thought, desire, word, and action so heinous. For those who have been the recipients of His gospel love, grace, and mercy, it is reason to weep—that our hearts would be against the God who is for us in Christ! This is the Thai boy, having been carried out of the miserable cave in the strong arms of his rescuer, responding by slapping his rescuer across the face.

Before glorification, every Christian will fall prey to such madness. Though we are no longer in the flesh, the flesh remains in us. This anti-God principle within is the result of our fall in Adam, which is why David confesses not only his actual sins but also his original sin: "Behold, I was brought forth in iniquity, and in sin my mother conceived me" (Ps. 51:5). We are born in sin, and even after we are born again by grace, we continue to struggle with evil desires that are against our Lord. Our arrogance, greed, covetousness, laziness, gluttony, lust, rage, and prayerlessness flow from a sinful principle within that hates God. It ought to lead us to mourn with David, and to the degree we know God, it will. If we treat our sin lightly, it is because we have a lightweight god. But as the weighty glory of God presses down on our souls, we see just how grotesque and insane our sin really is.

Attempting to hide our transgressions from God and others only heightens our misery. Given that God has revealed Himself to be "the LORD, the LORD God, merciful and gracious, longsuffering, and abounding in goodness and truth" (Ex. 34:6), there is joyous freedom that comes from bringing our sins in all their ugliness before Him. David is restless to do this. He's tired of hiding. Are you? Has the weight of God's moral beauty descended on your soul in such a way that to harbor your sin within is unthinkable? Confession of sin is a merciful, loving, gracious gift to wilderness pilgrims like us.

If you ever find yourself in Chattanooga, Tennessee, you are warmly welcome to Lord's Day worship at Cornerstone Presbyterian Church. Our morning service always begins the same way. God calls us to worship and greets us, and we respond in prayer and praise. God then convicts us of sin through the reading of His law, and we respond by confessing our sins. Every Sunday this is what happens because our worship roughly follows the divinely revealed liturgy for public worship in the old covenant tabernacle-temple (see Leviticus 9). Following God's call, old covenant worship began with a sin offering for the sinful priests and the sinful people. God's sinful people needed to freshly grapple with their sin in all its heinousness as they renewed covenant with God. Sin is so serious that it warrants death. But God is so good that He spills the blood of a substitute in the place of His people so that they may be ushered into covenantal communion with Him in His mercy, love, and grace. This is why after confessing our sins against God in public worship, He then assures us of pardon in Jesus Christ.

I often imagine it like this. The hospitable God invites us to His house in the call to worship. When we arrive in response to His loving invitation, He embraces us at the door in gospel grace and peace by way of the greeting. But then, in the call to confess sin, He quickly pulls us back and takes a look at us, saying, "You are filthy! Where have you been all week?" We look at ourselves and suddenly realize we are a mess, causing us to cry out for a fresh display of divine mercy in the prayer of confession. God then responds by washing us clean as He brings us beyond the entryway to enjoy intimate fellowship with Him in His house with the assurance of pardon.

God does this every week because we need it every week. In fact, what God does in public worship is a corporate display of what you and I need every day. Who among us has ever loved and served God like He deserves to be loved and served? In this wilderness, we fail every moment to live entirely for God because there is a tireless principle of evil in us that is against God. So, time and again God convicts in order that time and again we can confess. It is as we restlessly pursue mercy that we obtain it and thereby make spiritual progress.

Desperate Clinging to God for Pardon
Having confessed his sin, David is hungry to be assured of

God's pardon and forgiveness: "Purge me with hyssop, and I shall be clean; wash me, and I shall be whiter than snow" (Ps. 51:7). Like the prodigal coming forth from a pigsty, David is stinky and sullied with sin. But like the priests sprinkling water on the unclean with their hairy-leafed hyssop branches, David brings his dirty soul to the God who can make him clean, praying, "Hide Your face from my sins, and blot out all my iniquities" (v. 9). It is a graphic picture of God's salvation, treating David as if he has never sinned. Elsewhere David revels in this gospel reality as the spring of blessedness:

> Blessed is he whose transgression is forgiven,
> Whose sin is covered.
> Blessed is the man to whom the LORD
>   does not impute iniquity,
> And in whose spirit there is no deceit. (Ps. 32:1–2)

Knowing such blessedness, David now seeks the fresh realization of it.

But that raises a question. The gospel blessing of justification is a one-time act of God wherein He pardons our unrighteousness—past, present, and future—and imputes to us the righteousness of Christ. Through our union with Christ, we are liberated on the basis of Christ's finished work from the guilt of every sin we have committed or ever will commit. "There is therefore now no condemnation to those who are in Christ Jesus" (Rom. 8:1). Given our once-for-all justification and the once-for-all sacrifice of Christ as our wrath-satisfying, guilt-atoning sin bearer, is David's prayer really appropriate for us to pray? If every sin we will ever commit is already blotted out through Christ's blood and righteousness, then is it not a fundamental denial of the gospel to pray for pardon and forgiveness?

Jesus didn't seem to think so. In His model prayer given to His disciples, He taught them to pray, "Forgive us our debts" (Matt. 6:12). This is not the cry of an unconverted heathen toward God as angry judge; this is the cry of an adopted child toward God as loving Father (v. 9). Our Lord taught His believing followers to ask their fatherly God for forgiveness. Furthermore, this petition for forgiveness is syntactically connected to the previous petition for God's daily provision of our physical needs (v. 11). We need daily forgiveness just as much as we need daily bread, and there is only one place to go for both—our heavenly Father.

When David prayed for God to blot out his sins, he was not praying to be justified yet again. When we cry out to the heavenly Father for forgiveness, we are not praying to be adopted again. What are we doing then? We understand that sin disrupts the best of relationships, even though it may not destroy that relationship. When my son sins against me, I don't un-son him. I don't kick him out of the house and tell him he is no longer a part of the family. But his disobedience does disturb the peace and joy of our relationship. It warrants a righteous anger on my part, along with corrective discipline. That fatherly discipline is to the end of his owning his sin and asking for forgiveness in order that he and I may be reconciled. This is the kind of pardon we are seeking from God when, as justified children of God, we pray, "Father, forgive us." Our sin doesn't destroy the relationship, but it does disrupt it. Thus, we seek our Father's loving removal of that unrest. We have disobeyed Him, and we are coming to Him with our sinful defiance, seeking His warm embrace and assurance that He has made provision for even this sin and will never cast us out. We are not looking to be justified again but to be reassured of our justification.

In its continual struggle with sin, the healthy soul restlessly desires a deeper experiential grasp of Christ's sin-atoning death and law-abiding life. This is blessedness, indeed, as the soul feasts perpetually on God's gracious pardon in "joy and gladness" (Ps. 51:8).

Desperate Clinging to God for Power

None, however, can know God's gospel pardon without also knowing His gospel power, for the Christ who makes atonement for our sin as priest is the Christ who subdues us to Himself as king. David's hungry soul continues, "Create in me a clean heart, O God, and renew a right spirit within me" (Ps. 51:10 ESV). His spirit—the innermost core of who he is—needs radical reordering. His soul is a mess with misplaced priorities and fleshly desires. He needs an extreme soul makeover. Have you ever felt that way? I find myself praying this petition all the time in a variety of situations:

- It takes only one news headline, and my heart is in the grip of carnal fear. "Renew a right spirit within me, God!"

- It takes only one person to cut me off on the highway, and my heart is in the grip of murderous rage. "Renew a right spirit within me, God!"

- It takes only one compliment after a sermon, and my heart is in the grip of arrogant self-exaltation. "Renew a right spirit within me, God!"

- It takes only one advertisement flashing before my eyes, and my heart is in the grip of materialistic greed or adulterous lust. "Renew a right spirit within me, God!"

This is the restless cry of the believer, who, in this present age, faces a perpetual struggle with remaining sin. David doesn't just want to be forgiven for his heinous acts, but he wants God to change him so that he doesn't stray like this again.

He is longing for a holy heart that is a fit habitation for the Holy Spirit: "Do not cast me away from Your presence, and do not take Your Holy Spirit from me" (Ps. 51:11). Just as believers cannot lose their justification, so, too, believers cannot lose the Holy Spirit in the ultimate sense. But Christians can "grieve" and "quench" the Spirit (Eph. 4:30; 1 Thess. 5:19). Our sin and unbelief stifle His gracious influence in our souls. It keeps us from enjoying ever-deepening fellowship with Him through fresh infillings of His sanctifying person. David wants as much of the Holy Spirit as a pardoned sinner can possibly have.

Here is one grand motivation to ache with discontented desire for sanctification: If you are in Jesus Christ, you are the Holy Spirit's dwelling place (1 Cor. 6:19). Those who love God and marvel at His gracious indwelling want to make for Him the most beautiful, orderly house possible so that He will be pleased to fill it with all of His fullness. The more He fills us, the more His holy desires prevail against the unholy desires of the flesh, causing us to make progress in reflecting the God we have been recreated to image in Christ.

Can you think of greater joy than that? When we

stumble and seek our joy in the world's trinkets, let us pray in earnest, "Restore to me the joy of Your salvation" (Ps. 51:12). Let us seek an expanding experience of this redemptive joy through our Lord Jesus.

Desperate Contrition Under God's Delight

Those who are in Christ ought to be the happiest people on the planet! What is joy but living under the bright countenance of God, which is precisely what David tells us the contrite, Christ-exalting heart does:

> The sacrifices of God are a broken spirit,
> A broken and contrite heart—
> These, O God, You will not despise. (Ps. 51:17)

God didn't take pleasure in the heartless ritual of animal sacrifices under the old covenant. His delight was in the heart that offered up those sacrifices while genuinely declaring, "This is what my heinous rebellion deserves. I should be slaughtered for my treason against God. My neck should be broken and my blood poured out. But God, in His gracious mercy and love, has provided a Lamb to be broken and pierced in my place, and I cling to Him as my only hope."

Is that your heart? Because if it is, then the beaming countenance of God's glorious face shines on you. Rather than despising such a heart, He delights in it. It is not our sinless perfection that guarantees His smile; it is Christ who guarantees His smile. The heart that is conscious of its continual struggle with sin so that it is continually hankering after more of Christ's pardon and power is a heart that is blessed. As Jesus said,

He who loves Me will be loved by My Father, and I will love him and manifest Myself to him.... If anyone loves Me, he will keep My word; and My Father will love him, and We will come to him and make Our home with him." (John 14:21, 23)

God with us is blessedness, and God makes His home with and manifests His glory to those who live on and love the Savior.

You probably know a married couple who are disproportionately matched. The wife is godly, beautiful, smart, organized, funny, and good with finances. But the husband is the exact opposite of all those things. It leads you to ask (not out loud, of course), "How did he get her? What could have possibly led her to covenant herself to him for life?"

There is no match with a more glaring disproportionality than God's marriage to His people. As we set our finitude against His infinitude, we realize there is a boundless ontological disproportion between us. But if that is not enough, we then set our fallenness against His holiness and realize there is a boundless ethical disproportion between us. Why would God covenant Himself for all eternity to corrupt creatures of the dust like us? The only answer we are given is *love*. In our finitude and filth, He mysteriously sets His free affection on us, an affection so incomprehensibly vast that He sacrificed His infinitely valuable Son to win us back. He gave Christ to redeem us from our idolatry so that we could be restored to a loving communion bond with Him.

This is the gospel, and we never outgrow our need of it or plumb its depths. In our wilderness struggle with sin, we are restless for fresh assurances of Christ's love and applications of His saving benefits.

It is this gospel restlessness that delivers us from the twin errors of legalism and antinomianism. The legalist fails to live in light of Christ's pardon. The antinomian fails to live in light of Christ's power. But both have the same deadly root—a failure to see and savor God's goodness displayed in His gospel mercy and love that reaches down to deliver us from sin's condemnation and corruption. There is no easier way to kill biblical spirituality than embracing these deadly errors, and there is no other way to kill these deadly errors than to be continually laying hold of Christ in His pardon and power.

Complacency makes us smug in our sin, but the godly soul aches for an ever-deepening experience of divine rescue through the Son of God, driving him to the large-hearted God and His saving word with desperate desire.

If that does not result in spiritual progress, then I don't know what does.

CHAPTER 4

Restless for God's House

My soul longs, yes, even faints
For the courts of the LORD;
My heart and my flesh cry out for the living God.
—PSALM 84:2

On March 19, 2020, California became the first state to respond to COVID-19 by issuing a stay-at-home order. Unless your work was deemed essential or there was an essential need that required leaving your personal residence, you were ordered to stay home. Other states quickly followed suit, and the church quickly found itself legally prohibited from assembling since its service to God in public worship was deemed by certain civil authorities to be nonessential. In the promotion of public health, the doors of the church were closed, and live stream became the new norm. Without getting into whether this was a legitimate use of civil authority or whether live streaming Lord's Day worship services is a legitimate use of technology, what is most troubling, looking back, is how content many professing Christians were to stay home on Sunday and watch a live stream of a worship service. It revealed that, by and large, we don't believe something altogether unique is taking place when God's people assemble as His holy temple on His holy day to bask in His holy presence. There was a disturbing lack of restless aching to return to the house of God.

The heart that longs for God will long for the place where God's glory dwells. The heart that longs for God's word will long for the place where that word is expounded and applied. The heart that longs for God's salvation will long for the place in which gospel grace is offered in rich abundance.

But Isn't God Present Everywhere?

While God is the immense and omnipresent Lord and fills every place, He sovereignly chooses to manifest His covenantal glory in particular places. Under the old covenant, the place of His choice was the tabernacle-temple. Israel was not to offer up their sacrifices in just any place, but only at "the place where the LORD your God chooses, out of all your tribes, to put His name for His dwelling place" (Deut. 12:5). While the entire land of Canaan was a garden-temple wherein God communed with His people, there was a particular place among the tribes where God dwelled and public worship was carried out—the pre-Solomonic tabernacle and the post-Solomonic temple. This is the place that the psalmist, a temple musician, is panting after with intense desire: "My soul longs, yes, even faints for the courts of the LORD" (Ps. 84:2).

A similar confession of wilderness discontent comes from a temple servant, who, when providentially separated from God's house, exclaims,

> As the deer pants for the water brooks,
> So pants my soul for You, O God.
> My soul thirsts for God, for the living God.
> When shall I come and appear before God?
>   (Ps. 42:1–2)

This temple servant assumes that God is present to hear his prayer. So why is he thirsty for the divine presence if he already has it? Why does he ask, "When shall I come and appear before God?" if he is already before God? This son of Korah understands something that we too easily forget—God is everywhere present, but He is especially present in particular places and at particular times. From the Hill Mizar the psalmist can pray to God and worship Him privately (v. 6), but nothing can replace assembling on Mount Zion with God's holy people on God's holy days in God's holy presence, for it is there that God is pleased to dwell in His august glory.

The old covenant tabernacle-temple with its priesthood and sacrificial system was a shadow of better things to come. God's house is no longer a physical structure on a physical piece of property (John 4:20–24), for at His first coming, Christ began a temple-building project not using marble and mortar, but redeemed, flesh-and-blood people. The church, locally and universally, is God's tabernacle-temple (Eph. 2:19–22). Through their union with Christ, believers are the living stones comprising the temple, the living priests serving in the temple, and the living sacrifices offered up in the temple (1 Peter 2:4–5; Heb. 13:15–16; Rom. 12:1, respectively). God's new covenant house is the corporate assembly of His eternally loved blood-bought people. While we can experience the gracious presence of God in both private and family worship, there is no place God delights to manifest His glory like public worship, when His people gather together as His holy dwelling place. The six days we spend journeying through this wilderness world each week ought to make us pant after "the habitation of [God's] house, and the place where [His] glory dwells" (Ps. 26:8).

After Tessa and I have lived together for over a decade, imagine if I was forced to relocate to another place but was unable to bring Tessa along. Every day we connect with each other through FaceTime, and after a few weeks, I think to myself, *You know, this really isn't so bad. Tessa and I can still maintain our relationship, and a FaceTime marriage gives me more time for me. I get the benefits of marriage without it consuming my life.* What would such thoughts reveal? They would expose that I never really drank deeply from the fount of face-to-face, skin-to-skin, heart-to-heart marital intimacy. Anyone who knows the sweetness of the physicality of the marriage relationship will not be content with a FaceTime marriage. The distance will provoke intense longing. To go months without physically assembling in God's special presence, content to watch a live stream from the couch, is like a husband who is content to maintain his marriage through an iPhone screen. There are times when Tessa and I are forced to be away from each other, and there may be times when we are providentially hindered from assembling with God's people (like the psalmist), but the healthy soul is never satisfied with that.

Desiring God's Holy House

Psalm 84 is a love poem to the house of God. "How lovely

is Your tabernacle, O LORD of hosts!" (v. 1). Here is the only time in the entire Old Testament where the Hebrew adjective *lovely* is applied to an impersonal object. It is the adjective God uses to describe His people when He calls them His *beloved*. The temple is the psalmist's beloved. He treasures this house with his innermost affections. But so that we don't suppose the psalmist is falling prey to idolatry (i.e., worshiping a physical building that is part of the creation), like we might have thought in Psalm 119, he makes clear that his love for the temple is not because of its beautiful architecture, sweet-smelling incense, or gold furniture. Why does the psalmist love this house? The answer is found in those two words "Your tabernacle." The tabernacle is beloved because it is the hallowed residence of this man's Beloved. The house is lovely because it belongs to the God he loves. His longing for God's house is an expression of his longing for God Himself, for the temple is where the thrice holy One displays His unparalleled beauty.

We see it again in the aching petition of a son of Korah driven far from the tabernacle in wilderness exile:

> Oh, send out Your light and Your truth!
> Let them lead me;
> Let them bring me to Your holy hill
> And to Your tabernacle. (Ps. 43:3)

This man is suffering the darkness of external oppression and internal depression. He needs divine light to direct his steps back to the house of God. He is overwhelmed with lies as his enemies and his own soul conspire together, saying,

"Where is your God?" He needs divine truth to expel the falsehoods and direct him back to the house of God.

There is nothing but dwelling in God's special presence on God's special hill at God's special time that will satisfy his thirsty soul:

> Then I will go to the altar of God,
> To God my exceeding joy;
> And on the harp I will praise You,
> O God, my God. (Ps. 43:4)

Turn that phrase over in your mind: "God my exceeding joy." Can you genuinely say that? The golden crispness of a fall morning gives you joy. The smooth boldness of a hot cup of dark roast gives you joy. The little arms of your son or daughter wrapped tightly around your neck gives you joy. The belly laughter shared with a close friend gives you joy. But all these joys are derivative joys pointing to your ultimate joy. Is God the joy that exceeds and infuses every other joy? If He is, His holy house will be a most desirable destination.

What motivates you to get out of bed on Sunday to gather with God's people? We certainly ought to delight in fellow believers and desire their fellowship (Ps. 16:3). We ought to desire and delight in the physical rest from our vocational labors after a strenuous week (Mark 2:27). But the chief motive that should drive us with longing to God's new covenant house is God Himself.

Desiring God's Hospitable House

If I received an invitation to a presidential state dinner at the White House, I would immediately conclude that some wisecrack was playing a joke on me. An average, relatively uninteresting American like me doesn't get invited to dine with the president at his house. God, however, is not like the president of the United States. Remarkably, He beckons the lowest and the least to come and feast with Him:

> Even the sparrow has found a home,
> And the swallow a nest for herself,
> Where she may lay her young—
> Even your altars, O LORD of hosts,
> My King and my God. (Ps. 84:3)

In His large-hearted hospitality, God has a place for even the birds in His house. If He makes room for the sparrows that are neither the image of God nor the sons and daughters of God, how much more will He ensure there is room for us (see Christ's argument from the lesser to the greater in Matthew 6:25–34). God welcomes us in Jesus Christ, sinful and weak though we be (Rom. 15:7).

The hospitality of our divine Host makes His house all the more desirable. I might be excited to take a weekend trip to Washington, DC, to tour the White House, but how much more eager (and amazed) would I be if I received a loving invitation from the president himself to spend the weekend with him? There is no greater privilege in all the world than to be invited through the blood-splattered altar into the inner sanctum where God's glory is revealed. It ought to astound us every time we hear the call to worship. What amazing grace! None of us deserve to be a part of His house. None of us deserve to have our souls satisfied with His beauty. If you feel unworthy, it is because you are! But through faith in our Great High Priest and Passover

Lamb, sinful earthlings like us come to Mount Zion and are beckoned to drink deeply from the infinite streams of God Himself.

The only sane response to this gracious welcome of our glorious God is praise: "Blessed are those who dwell in Your house; they will still be praising You" (Ps. 84:4). The praises of the saints are fueled by a sense of amazement that God would call them to Himself and embrace them in His love. No one grasping this mindlessly mumbles psalms and hymns. The heart that is amazed at God's gracious invitation in Christ will erupt in joyous, adoring, awestruck praise:

> O what wonder! How amazing!
> Jesus, glorious King of kings,
> Deigns to call me his beloved,
> Lets me rest beneath his wings.
> (Mary D. James, "All for Jesus")

Desiring God's Heartening House

Our journey through this wilderness world saps us of our spiritual vitality. We live in what the psalmist calls "the Valley of Baca" (Ps. 84:6). *Baca* sounds like the Hebrew term for weeping. It is likely that the psalmist is not speaking of a physical location (since there is no archaeological or historical evidence of such a place), but figuratively referring to this world as a valley of tears. The saints live in a dry and weary land where they find nothing to drink except the tears streaming down their cheeks. But in this desert valley, there is a place where refreshing streams and pools of cool, crisp water can be found to hearten our weary, grief-stricken souls—Zion.

> Blessed is the man whose strength is in You,
> Whose heart is set on pilgrimage.
> As they pass through the Valley of Baca,
> They make it a spring;
> The rain also covers it with pools. (vv. 5–6)

This barren land is transformed into a fertile, well-watered land for God's pilgrim people as they fix their hearts on Zion and the God who dwells there. Though unable to live perpetually on God's holy hill, their hearts are always inclined there, and each time their hearts carry their feet to the divine house, their souls are revived in the presence of God. "They go from strength to strength; each one appears before God in Zion" (v. 7).

In public worship God sets before us a feast of rich food and drink, and the feast is nothing less than Himself. Through the ordinary means of grace—the reading and preaching of Scripture, the sacraments of baptism and the Lord's Supper, praying, and singing—God draws us into communion with Himself as "the God of all grace" (1 Peter 5:10). We call these elements *means of grace* not because they mysteriously communicate an ontological substance called grace, but because through them God reveals and offers Himself to us as the God who freely favors sinners in Christ. Through the fresh application of Christ's pardon and power in public worship, we encounter God and are strengthened as a result. We likely won't come out of God's house with bigger biceps (though sometimes our service to God is physically strenuous), but if we have truly engaged in the elements of worship with humble faith and reverent awe, our souls will be refreshed, strengthened, and fortified with God Himself as He prepares us to go back out into this desert world for another six days.

We need to be clear, however, that such soul strengthening comes only by engaging in the elements God has ordained. Aaron's sons, Nadab and Abihu, sought to approach God in His house by means of their own making, and instead of having their souls refreshed with life-giving streams, they were burned to a crisp in an all-consuming fire (Lev. 10:1–3). The Lord whom we worship is the Lord of His worship. We call this the regulative principle. In accord with the second commandment, the regulative principle teaches that God may be worshiped only through the elements He has commanded in His word, and any other possible means of worship are forbidden as idolatrous. Speaking of old covenant tabernacle worship, God said, "Whatever I command you, be careful to observe it; you shall not add to it nor take away from it" (Deut. 12:32). Those who delight in God and in His house are most zealous to ensure His house is not corrupted by man-made means. Funny skits, engaging cinematography, therapeutic homilies, dance routines—these and other machinations of man will leave the people of God dry and may even result in them being consumed in divine heat. God's house isn't a free-for-all. It's *His* house, and while He is a God infinite in grace, He is likewise a God infinite in glory. He is not to be trifled with.

But when the saints, with all their imperfections and weaknesses, approach God through Christ in dependence on the Spirit, engaging in the means He has ordained, their souls are filled and satisfied with the divine bounty.

We gather every week with hungry desire because

without this gathering our souls wither and die. This is why one of the strongest warnings in the Bible against falling away from Christ is prefaced by the command, "Let us consider one another in order to stir up love and good works, not forsaking the assembling of ourselves together, as is the manner of some, but exhorting one another, and so much the more as you see the Day approaching" (Heb. 10:24–25). It is possible to survive as a lone-ranger Christian, but it is not possible to thrive as a lone-ranger Christian. We need the strengthening that comes through the worship and fellowship we enjoy as God's gathered dwelling place. As our wilderness trials and temptations drain us of spiritual vigor, we must fix the eyes of our hearts with eager longing toward Zion.

Desiring God's Happy House

I sometimes joke that my great ambition as a pastor is that my church would be like a hole-in-the-wall diner. We've all been to one. You pull up, and your wife looks at you and asks, "Are you sure we are at the right place? There is no way a dump like this could have so many five-star reviews!" You assure her it is the right place and hesitantly walk in to find an aesthetically unpleasing room full of people who are having a delightful time. It is not until you take your first bite of food that it suddenly occurs to you why they are so happy to be there—for you have never eaten anything so delicious in your life!

My church meets in an unimpressive building, has a very ordinary pastor, is composed of very ordinary people, and is inherently lacking in programs and bells and whistles. You might pull up on a Sunday and think to yourself,

"Did I come to the right place?" But despite the unimpressive externals, my ambition is that there would be such a delicious feast of divine glory served up in public worship and such happy, Christ-exalting fellowship that first-time visitors would leave and say, "I've never feasted on the triune God like that! I'll be back for more and bring my friends too!"

A day is coming when God's new covenant temple will be externally glorious (Rev. 21:1–4). But as we await the not yet of Christ's consummated kingdom, our assembly looks incredibly ordinary, and that is because it is. When God, however, blesses His ordinary people through His ordinary means by His extraordinary grace, they experience a seven-course spiritual feast that leaves their souls fat with rejoicing. This is why the psalmist wants to be nowhere other than in God's house:

> For a day in Your courts is better than
> a thousand.
> I would rather be a doorkeeper in the house
> of my God
> Than dwell in the tents of wickedness. (Ps. 84:10)

He's happy to be the dishwasher as long as he can be there to feast on God!

Think about the most lavish place on the planet. The psalmist says he would gladly trade it one thousand times over to be in the tabernacle! The God who inhabits this house is blessedness itself:

> For the LORD God is a sun and shield;
> The LORD will give grace and glory.
> No good thing will He withhold

From those who walk uprightly.
O Lord of hosts,
Blessed is the man who trusts in You!
    (Ps. 84:11–12)

God is our sun, and it is in this place that the bright rays of divine favor shine on us. God is our shield, and it is in this place that we find divine protection and deliverance. Our love affair with the tabernacle is fueled by a longing after the blessedness of seeing, savoring, and serving the God of the covenant of grace.

It is no accident that God ordained public worship to reach its climactic conclusion with a benediction. When the pastor, as God's representative, raises his hands to prayerfully pronounce God's blessing, God is shining on His people. When Aaron declared the benediction in the very first tabernacle worship service, it resulted in nothing less than revival: "Then Aaron lifted up his hands toward the people and blessed them.... And the glory of the Lord appeared to all the people. And fire came out from before the Lord and consumed the burnt offering and the pieces of fat on the altar, and when all the people saw it, they shouted and fell on their faces" (Lev. 9:22–24 ESV). The benediction is no time to zone out as you think about the pot roast in the oven or the Monday morning meeting. It is no time to duck out of the service early. God is present with gospel blessing, and while we often assume He will show up most potently in the preached word, it may be that He will manifest His glory with knee-bending intensity in this holy pronouncement. Through the benediction, God puts His name on us (Num. 6:27). It is a triune name (2 Cor. 13:14), and it is the source of our joy and rejoicing, for God is saying to us, "I am yours, and you are Mine! As you journey through another wilderness week toward your promised rest, there is nothing you will face that can separate you from My holy love!"

Wooed to Worship

God gives us psalms like Psalm 84 to woo us into His worship. He gives us an inspired song of restless delight for His house so that as we sing it, our souls will be stirred up to that very affectionate discontent.

How often I, as a pastor, have to remind myself of this. I can rebuke the complacent Christian all day long, saying, "Look, you really need to start making Lord's Day worship a priority. Don't you understand the fourth commandment? Don't you understand that live stream is no substitute for the physical, embodied assembling of the saints?" I can do that, and sometimes as a pastor I need to do that. There is a time for a loving smackdown. But how much better to ask the complacent Christian, "Can you explain to me anything in this world that could be better than gathering with God's eternally loved people in His glorious presence to magnify His great name and bask under His gospel blessing?"

The healthy soul recognizes there is nothing better. Healthy Christians, as long as they are providentially able, are eagerly present whenever the church's doors are open. Why? Because the Holy Spirit directs their hearts with delightful desire to Zion. In this desert of tears, they know there is a place their souls can be encouraged, emboldened, and transformed by the One whom their souls prize, and so they are restless for the house of God.

CHAPTER 5

Restless for God's Restoration

Restore our fortunes, O LORD,
like streams in the Negeb!
—PSALM 126:4 (ESV)

Micah was an Israelite by birth and quite a religious man. In the pursuit of blessedness, he built his own shrine (Hebrew for "a house of God"), crafted his own idols, and ordained his son to serve as his personal priest (Judg. 17:1–6). He was confident this would secure blessing, all without making him dependent on the actual house of God and its priests at Shiloh (18:31). But when Micah met a wandering Levite passing through Ephraim, the prospect of blessedness grew all the brighter. He offered this Levite an annual salary of ten shekels and a shirt to serve as his priestly mediator before his self-constructed idols in his self-constructed temple, and the Levite happily accepted his offer (17:7–13). But then a day came when Micah's priest got a better job offer. An entire tribe of Israel called him to be their priest with the promise of greater prominence and better pay. It was the promotion of his dreams, and he immediately took it, plundering his former boss in the process (18:14–20).

Who was this corrupt Levite promoting religious madness for self-serving ends? His name was Jonathan, and he was the grandson of none other than Moses (Judg. 18:30). Jonathan had heard his grandfather's preaching of the covenant on the plains of Moab. He had seen God fulfill His covenant promises in the conquest of Canaan. He was a member of the holy tribe of Levi, which had God Himself as their inheritance (Deut. 10:9). But Jonathan, despite his covenantal heritage and blessedness, had fallen away from the living God, making a living through the promotion of self-made religion in Israel.

The Natural Drift Toward Corporate Declension

If the book of Judges teaches us anything, it teaches us that God's people, left to their own devices, will always abandon the God they profess to love. The land of Canaan, which was intended to be an Eden-like garden where Israel delighted in communion with their God, became a desert of idolatrous rejection of God. Over and again throughout this inspired history, God's people follow a cyclical pattern of covenant breaking that looks like this:

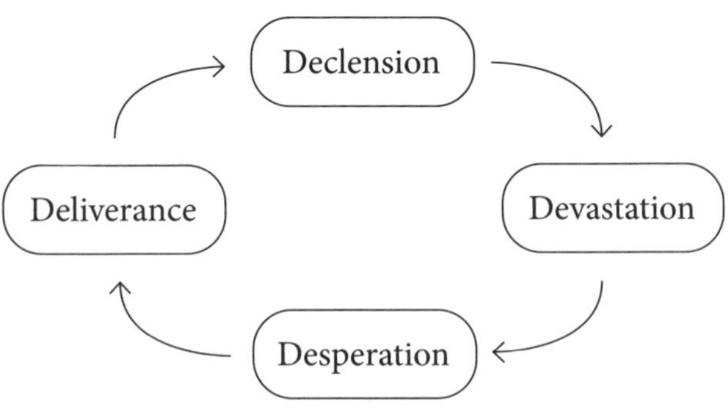

They forsake God, His word, His salvation, and His house. But it is no bare abandonment, for man must worship something, and so their forsaking the Lord is always an exchange of true religion for false. Israel trades the covenant God for creaturely idols, the covenant word for creaturely wisdom, the covenant salvation for creaturely works, and the covenant house for creaturely shrines. It is a declension that is nothing short of apostacy. That gross spiritual decline then leads to their devastation as God gives them over in judgment to the serpentine nations around them. Through that devastation, the people eventually come to their senses and turn to God, crying out to Him in desperation. God then responds by graciously raising up a judge who brings about deliverance. This is the cycle that occurs throughout the first sixteen chapters of Judges. As soon as a judge passes off the scene, Israel goes straightway into idolatrous declension again, running willfully into the devastation of covenant curse, which then leads them to desperation, resulting in a fresh display of divine deliverance.

What is the lesson? Apart from God's supernatural grace, His covenant people always drift into corporate idolatry, resulting in a forfeiture of covenant blessing. It is a lesson we mustn't forget lest we go the way of apostate Israel. If it can happen to the grandson of Moses, it can happen to any of us.

A Postexilic Lamentation

Such multigenerational declension among the old covenant people eventually led to the curse of exile as Israel was banished from Canaan under foreign domination.

First-time readers of the story assume exile must be Israel's final chapter. But even when God's people were grotesquely faithless, leading to divine divorce, God remained gloriously faithful (2 Tim. 2:13). He would come as Israel's Deliverer and restore them to the land in a renewed covenant bond. God promised this future restoration through His prophets:

> I will bring back the captives of My people Israel;
> They shall build the waste cities and inhabit them;
> They shall plant vineyards and drink wine from them;
> They shall also make gardens and eat fruit from them. (Amos 9:14)

> I will be found by you, says the LORD, and I will bring you back from your captivity; I will gather you from all the nations and from all the places where I have driven you, says the LORD, and I will bring you to the place from which I cause you to be carried away captive. (Jer. 29:14)

Even before the conquest of Canaan, Moses had foretold Israel's exile as the consequence of their idolatry. Yet in accord with the prophets to come, he assured them,

> Now it shall come to pass, when all these things come upon you, the blessing and the curse which I have set before you, and you call them to mind among all the nations where the LORD your God drives you, and you return to the LORD your God and obey His voice, according to all that I command you today, you and your children, with all your heart and with all your soul, that the LORD your God will bring you back from captivity, and have compassion on you, and gather you again

from all the nations where the LORD your God has scattered you. (Deut. 30:1–3)

Israel's declension would lead to the ultimate devastation, but when they came to their senses in repentant desperation, God would come again to deliver. A remnant of exiles would be gathered and restored to rebuild God's house and enjoy filial fellowship with Him in the land under a renewed covenantal bond.

What had been foretold by Moses and the prophets came to pass. In a remarkable display of sovereignty, God gathered a remnant of scattered exiles and restored them to the land of His favor. It is this event that the psalmist refers to as he recounts, "When the LORD brought back the captivity of Zion, we were like those who dream" (Ps. 126:1).

Psalm 126 begins on a happy note, but it is actually a lament. Lamentation is pain-provoked prayer that promotes praise. The circumstances giving rise to this postexilic song are not bright. For though a remnant has been restored to the land, Israel is in the darkness of spiritual declension. If you don't believe me, just read the postexilic prophets. Haggai, Zechariah, and Malachi expose and rebuke the returnees for their complacency and corruption. When they should have been sacrificially building God's house, they were watching HGTV and obsessing over their own houses: "Is it time for you yourselves to dwell in your paneled houses, and this temple to lie in ruins?" (Hag. 1:4). God blessed the ministries of Haggai and Zechariah, working repentance in His people and encouraging them to finish building the second temple under the leadership of Zerubbabel. But no sooner was

His house complete than it became full of such religious corruption that God desired its doors to be permanently shut and its offerings to be permanently discontinued:

> "Who is there even among you who would shut
>   the doors,
> So that you would not kindle fire on My altar
>   in vain?
> I have no pleasure in you,"
> Says the LORD of hosts,
> "Nor will I accept an offering from your hands."
>   (Mal. 1:10)

We aren't given an inscription in Psalm 126 that indicates exactly when during Israel's postexilic history it was written. But whether it was in the days of Haggai and Zechariah, as the second temple sat in ruins, or in the days of Malachi, as the second temple stank with corruption, what is clear is that God's postexilic people were in a spiritual condition that warranted lament. Not just any lament, mind you, but corporate lament (see the pervasive use of plural verbs and pronouns throughout the first five verses). To return to the cycle of Israel's covenant breaking, Psalm 126 is an expression of desperation birthed out of devastation resulting from declension.

Remembering God-Exalting Laughter in the Past

So why is the first note of this song a happy one? It is because in the midst of desperate circumstances, the psalmist is remembering God's past deliverance: "When the LORD brought back the captivity of Zion, we were like those who dream" (Ps. 126:1). Many of the Jews had been born in captivity. All they knew was enslaving bondage to Babylon for decades on end. When God delivered them, it was so shockingly wonderful that they kept pinching themselves to make sure it wasn't all a dream.

God's unbelievable restoration resulted in unspeakable joy and rejoicing: "Then our mouth was filled with laughter, and our tongue with singing" (Ps. 126:2). This is the underdog scoring the winning touchdown of the championship game and bursting forth in a happy roar. No one saw this coming, and the shocking, unexpected nature of it warrants laughter. But unlike the underdogs who flexed their muscles and patted one another on the back as they exulted in their victory, Israel's celebratory astonishment is directed toward God. It was the Lord who restored them, and this was so obviously the case that even the pagan nations confessed it to be so: "Then they said among the nations, 'The LORD has done great things for them'" (v. 2). The psalmist leads Israel to concur with the nations: "The LORD has done great things for us, and we are glad" (v. 3). While the nations were forced to admit God's mighty deliverance of His exiled people, they were strangers to the experiential joy of that deliverance. These returned exiles, on the other hand, were the objects of this deliverance and thus experienced the gladness of such lavish liberation.

This hardly sounds like lament, but it is. For it is against the backdrop of the God-exalting laughter of past days that the psalmist sees the present godless, lamentable condition of the people. When we forget the past, it is very easy to grow complacent in our spiritual declension and devastation. We settle for spiritual compromise in our souls, coldness toward God's worship, and a lack of zeal for God's kingdom. We come to expect preaching to be dull and powerless, evangelism to be unfruitful, and prayer meetings to be lacking in attendance and earnestness. We look at the American church more broadly with its seeker-sensitive rejection of the cross, its man-exalting celebrity culture, and its exchange of the gospel for social justice, and we throw up our hands in hopeless resignation. This is just the way it is, right? Shouldn't we expect little holiness with much compromise, little of the divine presence with much impotence, and little reformation with much deception? The answer is yes if the church is left to its own devices, for God's covenant people always drift toward spiritual declension and idolatry. But the history of God's people makes plain that we ought not to settle for the devastation of our foolish idolatry as normal because God is with us, in us, and for us in Jesus Christ.

This is one grand reason why early in my pastorate I preached through the book of Acts. I saw in my own heart and in my congregation a complacency that needed to be countered by an experiential remembrance of the past. Luke's inspired history records a unique, redemptive-historical moment as the risen Lord Jesus lays the apostolic foundation of His church. Thus, not everything set forth in Acts is normative for the life of the church today (e.g., the apostolic and prophetic offices with their accompanying signs and wonders). But the Holy Spirit's ministry of powerfully blessing the proclamation of His word for the salvation of sinners and the sanctification of saints is not something reserved for the apostolic era. If we read this history rightly (along with the history of old covenant Israel), we won't be able to remain complacent with little of the presence and power of God in our midst. Seeing the past blessedness of God's people, we will lament our present sorry state and long for brighter days under God's restorative grace.

There is no better way to learn how to pray than through the inspired prayers of Scripture. If you study the great revival prayers in the Bible, you will find they frequently begin by remembering the past. For example, the prayer for God's restoration in Psalm 85 begins by looking to God's past goodness:

> Lord, You have been favorable to Your land;
> You have brought back the captivity of Jacob.
> You have forgiven the iniquity of Your people;
> You have covered all their sin. (vv. 1–2)

Likewise, Isaiah's revival prayer for God's future exiles begins by harkening to the past, this time looking back to God's gracious deliverance in the original exodus:

> So He became their Savior.
> In all their affliction He was afflicted,
> And the Angel of His Presence saved them;
> In His love and in His pity He redeemed them;
> And He bore them and carried them
> All the days of old. (Isa. 63:8–9)

We cannot forget our history! Pastors and elders cannot fail to study the history of revival and reformation in the church's annals and share it with their people. We ignore the past to our peril. The God who time and again has restored the fortunes of His wayward people is ready and willing to do it again. But He waits to be sought after. He waits for His restless people to wrestle with Him in humble, believing prayer. He waits for watchmen on the walls of His renewed city to

> take no rest,
> and give [God] no rest
> until he establishes Jerusalem
> and makes it a praise in the earth.
> (Isa. 62:6–7 ESV)

Sadly, however, the exilic confession of Isaiah seems to be a fitting confession for our day: "There is no one who calls on Your name, who stirs himself up to take hold of You" (Isa. 64:7). As God's people, we must rouse our souls with the past so that we lay hold of God in the present with restless prayer for revival.

Embracing God-Exalting Lament in the Present

This is what the past remembrance of Psalm 85 leads to: "Restore us, O God of our salvation, and cause Your anger toward us to cease" (v. 4). It's the same cry as Isaiah's as he remembers the exiles: "Oh, that You would rend the heavens! That You would come down!" (Isa. 64:1). Eyeing God's past deliverance causes the church to pray, "Do it again, Lord!"

This is the logic of Psalm 126 as it shifts from remembering to petitioning: "Restore our fortunes, O LORD, like streams in the Negeb!" (v. 4 ESV). The psalmist pictures postexilic Israel in their worldliness and dead formalism as a dry wadi bed hardened by protracted drought. Does your soul ever feel that way? How about your church? The psalmist is not content for his soul and the souls of God's people to be a barren wilderness, so he pleads for God to send heavenly showers to drench this dry, hard, lifeless ground. The people of God have been living in spiritual drought for years, and he is longing for a torrential downpour of divine grace.

His longing is the longing of lament, which is provoked by painful, sorrowful, heart-breaking circumstances, and this is why he says,

> Those who sow in tears
> Shall reap in joy.
> He who continually goes forth weeping,
> Bearing seed for sowing,
> Shall doubtless come again with rejoicing,
> Bringing his sheaves with him. (Ps. 126:5–6)

The farming imagery would have resonated with the returnees, who lived in an agrarian society and depended on a fruitful harvest for their survival and prosperity. God's blessing is likened to a harvest that God's people are seeking after as they sow seed. As they cast the seed onto the desert ground, they are weeping. Their spiritual deadness and famine of experiential acquaintance with God causes them to agonize as they strive after Him. The hard ground beneath their feet is sprinkled with sanctified tears. What farmer is content with sowing seed and never having a rainstorm? Wouldn't months and years of drought cause him to agonize in desperation?

God's vineyard is supposed to be abundantly fruitful, but without rain nothing but desert thorns and thistles will grow. Are we content with that? Do we rest at ease, saying, "Well, I've been faithful. I sowed the seed, and now God can do whatever He wants"? Such thinking would have been foreign to Isaiah, who said in the midst of Israel's declension, "Look away from me, I will weep bitterly" (Isa. 22:4). It would have been foreign to Jeremiah, who likewise cried,

> Oh, that my head were waters,
> And my eyes a fountain of tears,
> That I might weep day and night
> For the slain of the daughter of my people!
>   (Jer. 9:1)

It would have been foreign to Christ, who lamented over the spiritual deadness of God's holy city (Matt. 23:37) and "offered up prayers and supplications, with vehement cries and tears" (Heb. 5:7), along with His apostle, who "did not cease to warn everyone night and day with tears" (Acts 20:31). These men didn't rest in their faithful sowing, content whether they reaped a harvest or not. They sowed with tears! There was a restless, discontented desire for God to come in blessing to restore His vineyard and make it glorious.

As pastors, can we be content just to faithfully expound and apply the Scriptures, sowing the seed of God's word, without seeing God use that preaching to bring forth abundant fruit?

As parents, can we be content just to instruct and discipline our children as the Lord calls us, without soaking our pillows in tears, asking God to bless our efforts for the salvation and sanctification of our own flesh and blood?

As witnesses, can we be content just to share the gospel with our neighbors in public without agonizing over their souls in private, pleading with God to effectually call them through His word?

What farmer in his right mind would ever rest with contented indifference toward the weather because he had sown faithfully? The rain must come, or the sowing is in vain!

We certainly must beware of a false emotionalism. But that doesn't appear to be much of a danger in Reformed ecclesiastical circles. Our danger is a lack of lamentation expressing a desperation for God to deliver, because apart from the floodwaters of His grace, this barren ground will produce nothing but wilderness thorns and thistles, even with all our faithful and diligent sowing. Have we forgotten how to lament? Do we have a place in our congregations for sackcloth, ashes, and weeping? Study redemptive history and church history, and you will find that whenever God is intent on moving in a mighty way to restore His people, He always stirs them up with brokenhearted, agonizing longing for better days.

I understand this is not a popular message today, but God's word won't allow us to airbrush flowers over famine. The clean-shaven, Sunday-best church culture we have created may be averse to lament, but if that is the case, then our church culture needs to change. This is not a call for gloomy congregational life and pastors who are all frowns; this is a call for the church and its leaders to realistically reckon with the spiritual condition of God's people and, to whatever degree is warranted, respond with the dissatisfied aching of lament.

The hungry soul that rouses itself to lay hold of God for restoration often expresses that hunger by forgoing physical food. Have you ever experienced sorrow in the midst of a tragedy that consumed your desire for physical food? Fasting is voluntarily abstaining from food as an expression of Godward agony and appetite. Jesus assumes His disciples will fast (Matt. 6:16–17). When asked during His earthly ministry why His disciples didn't fast, He responded with a wedding analogy: "Can the friends of the bridegroom mourn as long as the bridegroom is with them? But the days will come when the bridegroom will be taken away from them, and then they will fast" (Matt. 9:15). While Christ, the bridegroom, was present with His disciples, they feasted. But a time would come when He would depart, and then in the period between His ascension and His second coming, His disciples would fast. While a few of us may be physically unable to fast (if you are unsure, ask your doctor), we ought to be very slow to excuse ourselves from a practice that Jesus assumes and asserts is normal for His followers living between the already and the not yet of His kingdom.

Our fasting doesn't twist God's arm to do what He otherwise would not do. But if anything is clear from redemptive history, it is that when God's people return to Him with all their hearts by fasting, ordinarily God relents and pours out His grace. Such was the case with the corporate fasts in the days of Jehoshaphat, Ezra, Nehemiah, and Esther. Even the pagan city of Nineveh was delivered from God's judgment when they called a corporate fast to seek the Lord. Why? Because genuine fasting puts an exclamation point on the soul's agonizing appetite for God and His deliverance. When we sincerely fast, we are saying, "We are hungry for you, God! Our physical hunger has been eaten up by a hunger in our souls to see You working powerfully and dynamically in our lives, our church, and our nation!" Fasting is the soul's expression of humble earnestness before Christ, seeking His salvation as we await the final day of consummation.

In this wilderness, an individual believer or a corporate body of believers who never prays with tears and fasting is an anomaly, according to the biblical standard.

Who Knows What God Might Do?

In the face of national calamity, God called His wayward people,

> Yet even now…
>   return to me with all your heart,
> with fasting, with weeping, and with mourning;
>   and rend your hearts and not your garments.
>   (Joel 2:12–13 ESV)

This call to tear-filled, hungry, pleading, corporate lament is then followed by a most encouraging question. In fact, it is one of my all-time favorite questions in the Bible. Joel asks, "Who knows if He will turn and relent, and leave a blessing behind Him?" (v. 14). Given God's gracious character and His past dealings with His people, who knows what He might do? Our fasting can't strong-arm Him into blessing. It doesn't merit His blessing. We deserve His curse. But in light of who God has revealed Himself to be throughout redemptive history, the discontented brokenness by which we lay hold of God is wed to an eager expectation. We don't know when or how, but we are confident in this reality: "Those who sow in tears shall reap in joy" (Ps. 126:5). So we don't succumb to fatalistic pessimism regarding the sorry state of our soul, our family, our local church, or the broader church. As we prostrate ourselves before God in dissatisfied desire for a mighty outpouring of the Spirit to restore His people, who knows what our God might do?

CHAPTER 6

Restless for God's Mission

Let the peoples praise You, O God;
Let all the peoples praise You.
Oh, let the nations be glad and sing for joy!
For You shall judge the people righteously,
And govern the nations on earth.

—PSALM 67:3–4

We are living in dark days. No-fault divorce and the redefinition of marriage have struck deadly blows to humanity's most foundational institution. State-sanctioned abortion and euthanasia have resulted in the slaughter of untold millions of humanity's most vulnerable. The radical autonomy of transgenderism has led to the denial and mutilation of humanity's biological makeup. Atheistic evolution has popularized the rejection of humanity's Designer and dignity. Secular psychology and pornography have grossly sexualized humanity's fundamental identity and purpose. Critical theories have given rise to riotous rage and revolution among so-called oppressed classes, eroding humanity's fundamental unity. Political powers have waged an all-out war on religious liberty, disdaining one of humanity's fundamental freedoms and the God who gives it.

This is only a sampling of the darkness that pervades the wilderness world in which we find ourselves, and all of it is at root a willful failure on the part of humanity to see, savor, and serve the one, true, and living God. The spiritual darkness that pervades our nation and our world is the result of the fall of Adam. When Adam sinned, humanity fell in him. When Adam was kicked out of God's garden-temple for his covenant-breaking rebellion, humanity was banished from the light of God's life-giving, covenantal presence.

All of us would be in the dark were it not for the God of gospel grace. The history of redemption is the story of God reversing the effects of the fall through a second Adam. The gospel heralds a Christ who did not merely cancel the covenantal curse due to our unrighteousness but conferred to us the covenantal blessing due to His righteousness. What is that blessing? It is, as we have seen, nothing less than covenantal communion with God as our supreme treasure. Blessedness is basking in the light of God's countenance in the covenant of grace.

Between the already of Christ's inaugurated kingdom and the not yet of Christ's consummated kingdom, the people of God bask in this light while still remaining in a world under Adamic darkness. They, however, are not content with the darkness. The healthy Christian and the healthy church long for the soul-enlightening mission of Jesus to go forth in triumphant power for God's glory. This is the cry of Psalm 67.

The Missional Thrust of Godward Revival

When the covenant people of God seek to reach the world with the message of God's covenantal grace, where should they begin? Often churches, out of a godly zeal for the lost, make missions their number one priority. But the psalmist makes clear that while missions must always be a top priority for the church, it should not be the first priority, for missions is always the overflow of God's people seeing and savoring His bright, soul-satisfying glory. Genuine mission for God is the fruit of a deep devotion to God, His word, His salvation, and His house—a devotion that results from God's restorative grace. This is why, as the psalmist prays for God's worldwide mission, he begins by pleading for revival among God's people: "God be merciful to us and bless us, and cause His face to shine upon us" (Ps. 67:1). His longing echoes the priestly benediction:

> The LORD bless you and keep you;
> The LORD make His face shine upon you,
> And be gracious to you;
> The LORD lift up His countenance upon you,
> And give you peace. (Num. 6:24–26)

You probably have your name written on the inside of your Bible so that no one gets confused about who it belongs to. In the threefold pronouncement of "the LORD," God puts His name on us so that we don't get confused about who we belong to (Num. 6:27). Under the fuller revelation of the new covenant, that threefold pronouncement sounds like this: "The grace of the Lord Jesus Christ, and the love of God, and the communion of the Holy Spirit be with you all" (2 Cor. 13:14). God's singular name is a threefold name, and through the benediction He graciously brands His triune name on our souls. The experiential reception of God's name is the essence of spiritual life and vitality, and it is what delivers us from spiritual declension. As God's postexilic people discontentedly sang, "Restore our fortunes, O LORD, like streams in the Negeb!" (Ps. 126:4 ESV), so God's people with a zeal for the nations long for God's reviving face to beam on them and His reviving name to be indelibly stamped on them.

What does revival have to do with missions? Everything. The reason the psalmist prays for restoration among the covenant people is "that your way may be known on earth, your salvation among all nations" (Ps. 67:2). The fulfillment of God's international mission is the outworking of His bright blessing being freshly experienced by His holy nation. When God called idolatrous Abram out of darkness and into His marvelous light, He promised Abram,

> I will make you a great nation;
> I will bless you
> And make your name great;
> And you shall be a blessing. (Gen. 12:2)

God's blessing to Abram would result in Abram becoming a blessing not to a select few, but to "all the families of the earth" (v. 3). God's redemptive benediction would spread from Abram and his posterity to the nations. But the spreading necessitated that Abram's seed receive and relish in the blessing. To the degree they failed to do so, they would fail to spread it. How can you share something you don't possess? Before missions can happen, God-exalting, Christ-loving, worship-evoking spirituality must happen, for a revived church will be a body of compassionate, courageous, compelling, and consecrated witnesses.

True revival does not result in monkish retreatism

but actually moves the people of God outward in compassion toward the dark world. As the bright beams of God's glory shine on them through the compassionate face of Christ, they are transformed into Christ's likeness. Those who have the love of God filling their hearts love like God loves. How does God love? He pursues sinners in their misery in order to bring them into eternal blessedness. The refreshing streams of revival lead God's pursued people to lovingly pursue sinners, that they too may join in partaking of God's redemptive blessing.

That compassion is wed to courage because to live before the face of the reconciled God is to know deliverance from the fear of man. When the Spirit fills God's people, it results in bold evangelistic witness (e.g., Acts 4:31). Perhaps the greatest hindrance to our evangelism is the fear of man, but such is dealt a death blow when the soul is grappling with God in His supreme blessedness. For if we have the smile of Christ's Father beaming on us and the power of Christ's Spirit dwelling in us, what does it matter if the whole world frowns at and opposes us?

Furthermore, the revived people of God are delivered from duplicitous hypocrisy. The world can tell that they actually believe the message they proclaim and are willing to seal it with their blood if necessary. Along with that, the holiness of life that results from living under God's blessedness serves to "adorn the doctrine of God our Savior" (Titus 2:10). So because God's people speak with holy lips and lead holy lives, their witness is compelling.

Finally, the triune name effectually sealed on the souls of God's people causes them to no longer live for themselves but to recognize that in body and soul, they belong to God. As they compassionately, courageously, and compellingly take the light of God's gospel into the darkness of their neighborhoods, schools, workplaces, and beyond, they go as God's consecrated people—precisely the kind of people God delights to use in a mighty way!

Are you beginning to see why the spiritual vitality of the church, which is a fruit of God's reviving grace, must have priority over the church's mission? It takes God's powerful, enlivening, sanctifying, eternity-orienting presence to make a missional church. True revival always thrusts the people of God toward missions, resulting in the light of God's covenant blessing breaking into the darkness of the world around them.

The Worshipful Thrust of Godward Mission

The psalmist's restless desire for God's "salvation" to be manifested "among all nations" (Ps. 67:2) is at its core a desire for the glorification of God:

> Let the peoples praise You, O God;
> Let all the peoples praise You.
> Oh, let the nations be glad and sing for joy!
> For You shall judge the people righteously,
> And govern the nations on earth. (vv. 3–4)

As he looks at the godless nations around him, he longs for them to be reconciled to God through God's gospel word so that they may be pardoned and empowered to serve in God's house. What do redeemed sinners do in the house of God? They praise.

The chief end of the church's mission is the chief end of man—the glorification and enjoyment of God (see

Westminster Shorter Catechism 1). Contrary to fundamentalism, the chief end of missions is not getting people out of hell. Contrary to liberalism, the chief end of missions is not the alleviation of social ills. God wants to bring sinners under the bright beams of His gracious countenance in Christ so that they may worship Him as they were created to.

Worship is what missions is all about, which is why the first great commission, given to prefall Adam, was a call to multiply God's image until the whole earth was filled with God-exalting worshipers (Gen. 1:28). A closer examination of the creation account reveals that priestly Adam, with the help of his priestly posterity, was to expand the borders of God's garden-temple until it encompassed the globe. But that is precisely what Adam failed to do in his priestly pride, and so we find ourselves in a world full of people created to worship God who don't worship God. We live on a planet full of humans designed to bask under God's blessing and to bless Him in response who are instead under God's curse and curse Him in response.

How can the redeemed people of God possibly be content with that? Shouldn't it make us long? Shouldn't it bring tears to our eyes? Shouldn't it propel us to God in earnest prayer and fasting?

I am one of those "strange" individuals who finds immense pleasure in running. I love to run through the city in which I minister and pray Psalm 67 as I do. How quickly I can forget that the tens of thousands of people whom God has providentially placed in my backyard are all, without exception, created to glorify and enjoy God. As I run past the multitudes, I preach this to myself and rouse my soul to lay hold of God, asking Him to so move through His people bearing His word in Chattanooga that multitudes of God-hating sinners would be transformed through Christ into God-delighting worshipers. I pray for open doors for the gospel. I pray for Spirit-emboldened hearts to walk through those doors. I pray, "Let Chattanooga be glad and sing for joy in Christ! Make your saving power known through your weak people in this secularized city. Let the multitudes in this city praise you, God, as you recreate them through the gospel to affectionately exalt you!"

We tend to pray such small prayers, but Psalm 67 is a massive, universal, all-encompassing prayer. The people of God are crying out, "Fill the globe with happy worshipers! Bring to pass the glorious purpose for which you created the earth and the inhabitants in it! Cause Your saving power to spread through Your revived people so that all may exalt and enjoy You!" So long as there is a single person living on the planet who does not worship the true God, the psalmist is not content. Are we content with the neighbors around our churches largely being unchurched and unconverted? Or do we crave for all of our neighbors to affectionately exalt God's gospel beauty?

Our Lord, in accord with the psalmist, taught us to make the glorification and enjoyment of God the chief end of our praying. In what we call the Lord's Prayer, the very first petition, which has priority over all the others, is, "Hallowed be Your name" (Matt. 6:9). Jesus is teaching us to pray literally that God's name would be set apart as holy. It is the very name placed on us in the benediction. We aren't praying for God and His name to become holy, for He is infinitely, eternally, and unchangeably holy in Himself. Instead, we are praying that human hearts would reckon with His holiness and worship Him accordingly. Our glorification of God doesn't make Him glorious any more than your statement "Wow, that is massive" as you stand before Mount Everest adds a single speck of dirt to the mountain. When you write your wife a poem, praising her for her beauty, your words don't make her any more gorgeous than she is. When God is glorified by His people, nothing is added to His being. Instead, our souls are brought into alignment with the reality of His weighty being. According to Jesus, this is to be the first priority of prayer.

It is a priority we are to pursue throughout the whole earth. The prepositional phrase found at the end of the third petition, "on earth as it is in heaven," modifies all three of the preceding petitions. We are to pray that God's name would be hallowed "on earth as it is in heaven" (Matt. 6:10). How is God's name hallowed by the saints and angels in the heavenly realm? Heaven is a place of perfect and pervasive worship. The glorified saints don't have an exhaustive grasp of God's glory, for the finite can never contain the infinite, but they have a proper grasp of God's glory and a heart that rightly responds in delight-filled exaltation. Such is true of every glorified saint in the heavens without exception. As it is in heaven, so we are to seek it on earth in our own lives, our families, our churches, our cities, our nation, and our world. In concentric circles of ever-expanding concern, we are to pray that God, by His word and Spirit, would manifest His gospel glory, causing all to render Him the glory due His name.

What might happen if a revived church in the midst of grave international darkness began to pray like this? What might happen if instead of looking for the right apologetic proof or political candidate to bring our city, nation, or world into the light, we turned to the God of omnipotent grace and glory, asking Him to spread His worship?

When God is on the move, that is how His people pray. Every petition is subservient to this all-controlling desire for God's glory to overtake our lives and our world. Consider the final five petitions of the Lord's Prayer (Matt. 6:10–13). How do these serve the worship of God?

- We pray for God's kingdom to come, because the kingdom is the domain in which God's name is hallowed.

- We pray for God's will to be done, because holiness of life is the necessary fruit of seeing and savoring the glory of God and redounds to His glory.

- We pray for God to give us daily bread, because we need physical strength to glorify His name.

- We pray for God to forgive our sins, because our guilt makes us shrink back from His holiness and must be removed if we are to relish in His glory and joyously share it with others.

- We pray for God to keep us from temptation and sin, because such devilish idolatry is the failure to prize the holy God above all else.

Everything Jesus teaches us to pray for has its great end in worshiping God. Worship is the chief end of missions and the chief end of prayer, and the two are inseparably connected. For a church on mission that doesn't pray or a church that prays but is not on mission is a gross contradiction. Discontented desire for God's worship to spread will propel us to lovingly plead with our neighbors to come to Christ as we lovingly plead with God to bless His saving word.

The Fruit of Revival Praying and Bold Proclaiming

In the first century, God's holy nation was anything but holy. They were strangers to God's blessing, leading them to murder God's anointed King. But God, through their bloody folly, cut a new covenant by which He would restore them to Himself. Having delivered Christ from the grave and exalted Him to the heavens, God the Father endowed the glorified Lord Jesus with the Holy Spirit beyond measure (Acts 2:33). As Christ's tiny remnant of faithful followers gave themselves to persistent prayer, He responded by pouring out His resurrection Spirit on them like streams in the Negeb (1:12–2:13). Through the blessing of the Spirit, these revived Jews were empowered for bold gospel proclamation, which led to a massive crowd of apostate Jews being restored to fellowship with God through a new administration of the covenant of grace (2:14–41). Despite persecution, that restoration continued as multitudes of Israelites came to faith in God's messianic King, so that by the time we get to Acts 13, there are tens of thousands of converted Jews and Samaritans (half Jews) united to bless God for His blessing.

The thirteenth chapter of Luke's inspired history is the hinge on which the book of Acts turns. For these descendants of Abraham with the reconciled face of God shining on them are now propelled to take that gospel to the four corners of the globe as their leaders "ministered to the Lord and fasted" (Acts 13:2). They are earnestly seeking God through prayer and fasting, and as they do, God meets them and sets apart Paul and Barnabas for a mission to the Gentiles, without which we would not have the gospel in North America today. These men then respond with more fasting and praying before sending Paul and Barnabas on their way (v. 3).

Through the church's revival praying, these two weak, sinful Jews are emboldened and empowered to witness for Christ to the ends of the known world. As the gospel goes forth from their praying lips, idol-worshiping Gentiles are transformed into true worshipers. Everywhere Paul and Barnabas go, they establish outposts of God's kingdom (i.e., local churches) wherein God is affectionately exalted in Jesus Christ, always with fasting and prayer (Acts 14:23). The expansion of God's worship throughout the earth comes through restless disciples who express their hunger for God in fasting, their dependence on God in prayer, and their courage before God in costly evangelism.

The psalmist is confident that as the covenant people plead for revival with missional hearts and lives God will answer, fulfilling His great redemptive purposes: "Then the earth shall yield her increase; God, our own God, shall bless us" (Ps. 67:6). God will hear the restless cries of His people. Not a single one will go unanswered as His saving blessing circles the globe, causing human hearts to hallow Him. "God shall bless us, and all the ends of the earth shall fear Him."

The psalmist can be so certain because God's messianic King will get what He asked for:

> Ask of Me, and I will give You
> The nations for Your inheritance,
> And the ends of the earth for Your possession.
> 	(Ps. 2:8)

Our hope is not in the fervency of our praying, the frequency of our fasting, or the fluency of our evangelism. Our hope is in our heavenly King, who delights to use His people to advance His cause in this dark and depraved world.

Don't misunderstand what I am saying. Psalm 67 is not a formula to guarantee massive gospel expansion in your lifetime. God, in the mystery of His providence, often allows His prayer warriors and gifted evangelists to go years, decades, and sometimes even lifetimes without experiencing a great resurrection harvest. The psalmist wouldn't live to see what happened in the days of Christ and His apostles, but his prayer was answered in it. In fact, if you are a God-worshiping Christian today, the psalmist's prayer was answered when God regenerated your heart through the call of the gospel. The God to whom we pray "is able to do exceedingly abundantly above all that we ask or think, according to the power that works in us" (Eph. 3:20), and we have no idea how our restless cries and labors will be used in the grand scheme of His redemptive plan. It might not be until your funeral that the unbelieving family member for whom you prayed fervently will, in the wake of your death, wake up to the reality of the Christ you shared with him. It might be that God would answer our prayers for national repentance by hardening our nation in its sin so that it begins to more systematically persecute the church, leading to God's people being purified and God's gospel spreading as He takes what the enemy meant for evil and turns it into a shocking display of gospel goodness. God knows what He is doing, and not a single one of the restless cries of His missional people will go unheard or unanswered.

Restless for God's Mission?

Do you see that Thomas Edison, despite his deism, was spot on in his common-grace observation? The general truth that restlessness is the precondition of progress is particularly true when it comes to God's mission.

How does the light of God's gospel advance in this dark world for the promotion of God's worship? How are living stones, living priests, and living sacrifices added to God's new covenant house? How do the nations come to know the liberating pardon and power of Christ? God's ordinary means is very simple—a discontented people who delight in Him and His grace. Their Godward delight makes them restless for Him to be glorified in others and to share that delight with others in their sinful misery. Until the mission is complete and the kingdom is consummated, they cannot fathom sitting at ease in a stupor of indifference.

Many try to compensate for their lack of missional desire by reading another evangelism book or attending another missions conference. God can certainly use these means to stir up His people with genuine desires for the spread of His cause. But the fresh appropriation of God's bright countenance in the gospel, which leads to a missional heart, is often best found in the act of evangelism itself. Don't wait to witness until you feel like it. Witness when you don't feel like it, for as you share the good news, the beams of its blessed light will freshly shine on you.

As you share the good news, the animosity and hostility against the light will drive you to your knees in brokenhearted prayer to the only One who can overcome the darkness of unbelief. It is in the trenches that restlessness for God's mission is fostered, and that restlessness only intensifies when we see God respond by transforming miserable sinners into glad worshipers of Him in Jesus Christ.

CHAPTER 7

Restless for God's Vindication

Arise, O LORD,
Confront him, cast him down;
Deliver my life from the wicked with Your sword,
With Your hand from men, O LORD,
From men of the world who have their portion
  in this life.
—PSALM 17:13–14

In 2018 Wang Yi, the pastor of Early Rain Covenant Church, was arrested by Chinese police along with over one hundred members of his congregation. Yi was then sentenced to nine years in prison, and his wife was put under house arrest. The Chinese government installed surveillance cameras throughout the entire Wang home, robbing her of any semblance of privacy and forbidding her from having contact with family or church members. What was their great crime? They refused to embrace and propagate the anti-Christian dogmas of the communist state. Swearing ultimate allegiance to Christ, they would not obey the Chinese government when it required them to disobey Him.

In 2022 Deborah Yakubu, a young Nigerian student, was beaten to death and burned by Muslim extremists.

What was her crime? She had sent an internal message to her friends, praising Jesus for the help He gave her in her studies. She was charged with blasphemy and subjected to the most grotesque of penalties.

Yi and Deborah are two of a multitude of Christians in our day suffering imprisonment, torture, and death for the sake of Christ. And lest we think persecution is a reality only in Asia, Africa, and the Middle East, Christians in North America and Europe find themselves increasingly marginalized, vilified, and even criminalized for their biblical convictions.

Following God's Anointed Is Not Safe

Everywhere we go today, we are told, "Be safe!" Probably one of the most unaddressed cultural idols is physical safety. Given that God nowhere commands us to be safe nor promises us physical safety, it is sobering how quickly we Christians can begin bowing before the altar of safety, willingly disobeying God out of a sensed need to be safe. We certainly ought not to be reckless. We ought to wear our seatbelts when we drive, and our churches ought to have child protection policies and security protocols. But we need to understand that following Christ in this wilderness world is not safe. God speaks plainly, "Yes, and all who desire to live godly in Christ Jesus will suffer persecution" (2 Tim. 3:12). A godly life is one devoted to God, His word, His salvation, His house, His restoration, and His mission. When your soul is shaped according to Psalms 63, 119, 51, 84, 126, and 67, you can be certain that the devil and the world will rage against you.

This ought not to surprise us, for God tells us to expect

persecution, and perhaps nowhere more profusely than in the inspired songbook He has gifted to us. Psalms 1 and 2 introduce us to the Psalter's overarching message and philosophy of history. While Psalm 1 beckons us into blessedness through delightful reception of God's word, Psalm 2 calls us into blessedness through delightful submission to God's King. Sadly, both songs reveal that not every person chooses the path of blessedness. Many despise God's word and reject God's King, giving rise to two distinct peoples on the earth—the righteous and the wicked.

The wicked rage against God's King and all those who would swear allegiance to Him (Ps. 2:1–3). In fact, this is the main theme of the first book of the Psalter, as God's lowercase king, David, and his faithful followers struggle to establish his kingdom in the face of perpetual opposition. But what was true of David is ultimately true of God's uppercase King, Jesus Christ, and His faithful followers. (See the way the persecuted church prays Psalm 2 back to God in Acts 4:23–31.) The world rages against them as they seek to establish and advance the kingdom. As they do, they actually fulfill God's promise at the dawn of redemptive history. The first gospel preacher was God Himself, and His message was one of perpetual warfare between two seeds—the righteous children of God and the wicked children of the devil (Gen. 3:15). Until the consummation, this conflict continues to unfold as the godless nations rage against all who would swear allegiance to God's word and God's King.

The revived church of Christ that zealously engages in the mission of Christ will face opposition because of Christ. Why? Because true disciples, by their words and deeds, proclaim, "Jesus is Lord!" Their lips and lives manifest the reign of Christ, and nothing poses a greater threat to human autonomy or the totalitarian state than that. The wicked rage against the church because it, as the visible and audible manifestation of Christ's kingdom on the earth, assaults their devilish pride.

When the godly face verbal and physical abuse for Christ's sake, what ought it to provoke within their souls? Among other things, persecution ought to give rise to a Godward ache for ultimate vindication. The blows David takes from his enemies do not give rise to self-pity, murderous rage, debilitating anxiety, or hopeless despair. Instead, this wilderness hostility leads him to long for God to set things right.

Laying Hold of Our Divine Judge

David turns to his covenant God in lament, and he addresses God as the righteous Judge of all the earth:

> Hear a just cause, O LORD,
> Attend to my cry;
> Give ear to my prayer which is not from
> deceitful lips. (Ps. 17:1)

David wants God's righteous ear to hear his righteous case in order that divine justice may be executed: "Let my vindication come from Your presence; let your eyes look on the things that are upright" (Ps. 17:2). Like Yi, whose persecutors falsely charged him with government subversion, and Yakubu, whose persecutors falsely charged her with blasphemy, David is suffering an unjust verdict from his godless foes. This leads him to cry out with restless longing for divine vindication. He wants God to set things straight and bring the evil devices of his enemies to nothing.

David is innocent. Without claiming sinless perfection, he affirms that he is a man after God's own heart who is not guilty of the charges brought against him. Have you ever been falsely accused or suffered unjustly? David appeals to God, who knows the truth:

> You have tested my heart;
> You have visited me in the night;
> You have tried me and have found nothing;
> I have purposed that my mouth shall not
>   transgress.
> Concerning the works of men,
> By the word of Your lips,
> I have kept away from the paths of the destroyer.
> Uphold my steps in Your paths,
> That my footsteps may not slip. (Ps. 17:3–5)

Unlike the godless hearts of his persecutors, David's heart fears God. Unlike the lying lips of his persecutors, David's lips are free of deceit. Unlike the unrighteous ways of his persecutors, David's feet run in the path of God's commandments. God's anointed is saying, "My righteous heart, lips, and life are ever before You. So according to Your perfect knowledge and justice, rescue me from the injustice of the wicked!"

The divine courtroom is of far greater weight to David than the human courtroom. He shares the confession of the apostle in the face of unjust accusations: "But with me it is a very small thing that I should be judged by you or by a human court.... He who judges me is the Lord" (1 Cor. 4:3–4). The news headlines are painting him in the worst possible light, but David knows that ultimately the only thing that matters is what God thinks of him.

Here is a man with a clean conscience. He is not living in spiritual and moral compromise, and this is because his soul has been kept "by the word of [God's] lips" (Ps. 17:4). By faith in God's gracious promises, David has learned to walk in sincere obedience to God's righteous precepts. When the suffering we face is the result of our own godless folly, we can certainly look to God for mercy and grace. But only a clean conscience, washed in the blood of Christ and determined to do the will of Christ, can embolden us to lay hold of God for vindication as David does here.

Do you have such a conscience? Are you living on Christ's pardon and power? No person who is playing with sin and making excuses for moral compromise can pray like this. But when our imperfect yet sincere lives of obedience demonstrate that we are indeed the children of God, no longer walking in the path of sinners and sitting in the seat of scoffers, we are bold to come before God when "persecuted for righteousness' sake" (Matt. 5:10).

If our cause is just, then our cause is God's. We ought to restlessly seek after His vindicating verdict, crying out with those who have gone before us, "How long, O Lord, holy and true, until You judge and avenge our blood on those who dwell on the earth?" (Rev. 6:10).

Laying Hold of Our Divine Savior

David cannot reflect on God's judgment without reflecting on His salvation, for David's vindication will be his deliverance, and the only explanation for it is God's covenantal grace. What made him differ from his wicked enemies? Why did David delight in the word of God and do it? Why did he bend the knee before God's exhaustive lordship? It was all because of divine grace, and so too would be his future vindication. David lays hold of his divine deliverer, pleading, "Wondrously show your steadfast love, O Savior of those who seek refuge from their adversaries at your right hand" (Ps. 17:7 ESV). The persecution he faces has given rise to a desire for a fresh display of God's undeserved covenantal affection.

David is likely alluding to the exodus, when "the LORD saved Israel…out of the hand of the Egyptians" (Ex. 14:30), which then led the delivered people of God to sing,

> Who is like You, O LORD, among the gods?
> Who is like You, glorious in holiness,
> Fearful in praises, doing wonders?
> You stretched out Your right hand;
> The earth swallowed them.
> You in Your mercy have led forth
> The people whom You have redeemed;
> You have guided them in Your strength
> To Your holy habitation.
> (Ex. 15:11–13)

With His strong right hand, God had wondrously demonstrated His steadfast love by saving His people from their adversaries. Meditating on covenant history, David now looks to His covenant Savior with restless desire for a personal exodus. He continues,

> Keep me as the apple of Your eye;
> Hide me under the shadow of Your wings,

> From the wicked who oppress me,
> From my deadly enemies who surround me.
>   (Ps. 17:8–9)

God's king is praying God's word back to him. This is a personalized version of another song of Moses that exalted God for His loving care toward His wilderness people. God had found Israel

> in a desert land,
> And in the wasteland, a howling wilderness;
> He encircled him,
> He instructed him,
> He kept him as the apple of His eye.
> As an eagle stirs up its nest,
> Hovers over its young,
> Spreading out its wings, taking them up,
> Carrying them on its wings. (Deut. 32:10–11)

Like a mother bird keeps her chicks at the forefront of her vision and tenderly cares for them in their helpless state, God had kept Israel as the apple (literally, the pupil) of His anthropomorphic eye, protecting and providing for them throughout their wilderness journey. He did not do this because of anything in them but purely on the basis of His faithful, gracious, covenant-keeping love. As their Savior, He rescued them from their foes repeatedly. In his personal wilderness plight, David is crying out for God to do it again. He then bolsters his petitions for grace with a detailed explanation of his wicked foes, who look similar to the godless Egyptians and Moabites (Ps. 17:10–12).

It is clear that David's "delight is in the law of the LORD, and in His law he meditates day and night" (Ps.

1:2). The covenant word that had kept David's feet from stumbling is the same word that is fueling his pursuit of future salvation. The word was deep in his heart, and it is what kept him in these desperate times. Can such be said of us, who live after the exodus deliverance of Christ's cross and empty tomb? Is the history of God's covenantal deliverance so ingrained in our souls that when the world rages, it causes our hearts to burst forth in grace-exulting, deliverance-desiring, Bible-saturated prayers to the God of the exodus?

Laying Hold of Our Divine Warrior
The God who wiped out Pharaoh's armies in the exodus is a warrior God:

> The LORD is a man of war;
> The LORD is His name.
> Pharaoh's chariots and his army He has cast
>   into the sea;
> His chosen captains also are drowned in the
>   Red Sea. (Ex. 15:3–4)

David can't think of God's salvation of Israel through the exodus waters and the wilderness without pleading for God to unsheathe His sword and wipe out His unrepentant foes:

> Arise, O LORD,
> Confront him, cast him down;
> Deliver my life from the wicked with Your sword.
>   (Ps. 17:13)

He is calling on God to spill the blood of his foes as He drowned the Egyptians.

Such imprecatory prayers might make us squirm, but David is not squirming. In this redemptive-historical conflict, He wants the serpent's seed to be wiped out. It is his consistent prayer throughout the first book of the Psalter, including many of the psalms that precede this one.

> Arise, O LORD;
> Save me, O my God!
> For You have struck all my enemies on the
>   cheekbone;
> You have broken the teeth of the ungodly.
>   (Ps. 3:7)

> Pronounce them guilty, O God!
> Let them fall by their own counsels;
> Cast them out in the multitude of their
>   transgressions,
> For they have rebelled against You.
>   (Ps. 5:10)

> Arise, O LORD, in Your anger;
> Lift Yourself up because of the rage of my enemies;
> Rise up for me to the judgment You have
>   commanded! (Ps. 7:6)

> Arise, O LORD,
> Do not let man prevail;
> Let the nations be judged in Your sight.
> Put them in fear, O LORD,
> That the nations may know themselves to be
>   but men. (Ps. 9:19–20)

> Break the arm of the wicked and the evil man;
> Seek out his wickedness until You find none.
>   (Ps. 10:15)

May the LORD cut off all flattering lips,
And the tongue that speaks proud things.
    (Ps. 12:3)

Does anyone pray like this anymore? Is it even appropriate to pray like this in the wake of Christ's coming? Yes, as long as we remember that these imprecatory prayers are against Christ's unrepentant foes. We are not looking to God for vengeance out of a self-serving bitterness but out of a Christ-serving zeal. We want all who stand against Him, His word, and His church to be brought down. But we desire Christ's enemies to be brought down in repentance more than we desire them to be cut down in judgment. We call our persecutors to renounce their satanic rage against Christ and to bow the knee before Him and kiss Him (Ps. 2:11–12). If in their stubborn unbelief, however, they refuse to get low before His saving sovereignty, then we pray for God to render them what they deserve for their defiance and desecration of our Lord, His word, His salvation, and His house. We're not content with a world in which Christ is hated, His word is ridiculed, His salvation is mocked, and His house is defaced.

We pray, "Work repentance and faith in our persecutors like you have worked in us, but if they will not turn to Christ, then knock out their teeth and bring them into judgment for the sake of Christ's name!" We look forward to and hasten the day

> when the Lord Jesus is revealed from heaven with
> His mighty angels, in flaming fire taking vengeance
> on those who do not know God, and on those who
> do not obey the gospel of our Lord Jesus Christ.

These shall be punished with everlasting destruc-
tion from the presence of the Lord and from the
glory of His power, when He comes, in that Day, to
be glorified in His saints and to be admired among
all those who believe, because our testimony
among you was believed. (2 Thess. 1:7–10)

We don't blush with embarrassment at such a philosophy
of history. This is our hope! We plead with the wicked to
believe the saving message of God, but we also take comfort that God will eternally afflict those who unrepentantly
afflict us for the sake of Christ (2 Thess. 1:6). His coming in
judgment is the ultimate salvation of His believing people
at the hands of a wilderness world.

Dear reader, are you ready for the judgment to come?
Have you bowed your knee to and kissed the Son of God? A
day is coming when you will meet Him. He delays because
in His large-hearted mercy He desires you to repent so that
you will not meet His wrath. He offers to bring you through
the exodus waters of salvation and to make you the apple of
His eye in this wilderness world. He beckons you to willingly bow beneath His sweet scepter now lest He break
your knees on the last day with His rod of iron, forcing you
to grovel in the dust before His holy majesty. Christ will not
be trifled with, but He has made provision for your trifling
and mine so that the future judgment will be our ultimate
salvation and vindication! But you must humble yourself
before Him in repentant faith and believing repentance.

Our Heavenly Portion and Hope

The wicked outside of Christ ache with dread at the prospect of this great day, but the righteous in Christ ache with

desire for it. The wicked have their portion "in this life" (Ps. 17:14); hence, death and the judgment are greatly to be feared for they can take none of their earthly trinkets with them nor will they be able to hide behind their creaturely idols when they stand before God. On the contrary, the righteous do not fear death because their portion is not found in this fallen earth. Neither do they fear judgment because they have been made righteous in the Messiah. In his wilderness lament, this is where David ends: "As for me, I will see Your face in righteousness; I shall be satisfied when I awake in Your likeness" (v. 15).

The worst that David's enemies can do is kill him, but he knows that when he awakes from death he will be with God. God's king is looking to the future bodily resurrection immediately preceding the final judgment (e.g., Dan. 12:2). His body will be laid in the ground, but a day is coming when it will be raised and reunited with his soul to stand before God. Just as Christ's bodily resurrection was His vindication (1 Tim. 3:16), so too David's bodily resurrection will be God's consummate declaration that, contrary to the claims of David's foes, David is righteous and beloved through the Mediator of the covenant of grace. If that is not enough, David will, in the same moment, gaze on the face of God with glorified eyes and not be consumed. Instead, His vision of divine glory will usher him into perfect Godward transformation and Godward satisfaction forever. If that doesn't thrill your heart, you need to check your spiritual pulse!

David's hope is the hope of every believer and the reason why the apostle Paul, in the midst of perpetual persecution, did not lose heart: "For our light affliction, which is but for a moment, is working for us a far more exceeding and eternal weight of glory, while we do not look at the things which are seen, but at the things which are not seen. For the things which are seen are temporary, but the things which are not seen are eternal" (2 Cor. 4:17–18). A few years of suffering at the hands of a raging world is a light reality in comparison to the infinitely weighty glory of God the saints will enjoy everlastingly in Jesus Christ.

David's enemies might be successful in bringing him down to the grave, but even in the face of that bleak prospect, he confidently declares,

> For You will not leave my soul in Sheol,
> Nor will You allow Your Holy One to see
>   corruption.
> You will show me the path of life;
> In Your presence is fullness of joy;
> At Your right hand are pleasures forevermore.
>   (Ps. 16:10–11)

The God who delivered Israel by His right hand would deliver David and raise him up to the heavenly Zion, where he would experience comprehensive joy and unending pleasure at God's right hand. If you are in Christ, that is your hope! God did not abandon Christ to the grave but raised and exalted Him to His right hand as the firstfruits of a great resurrection harvest to come (1 Corinthians 15). David's wilderness afflictions evoked a discontented longing for that. Do ours?

Our Restlessness Put to Rest
One of my great joys as a pastor is premarital counseling.

I will often ask a couple in their first session, "How many days until the wedding?" Typically, without any forethought, they respond with great precision: "242 days, 7 hours, and 14 minutes to go!" I've never met an engaged couple that was content with being engaged. They are restlessly desirous for the wedding day, counting down the days and hours months in advance. The incompleteness of their relationship and the unique stresses of engagement make their hearts ache for covenant consummation. How much more does the church of Jesus Christ, which has been betrothed to the Lord but finds herself in the wilderness, long for the covenant consummation on the future horizon. It would be crazy not to long for the wedding day!

The consummation of all things marks the realization of all of our Godward longings here below.

- Our restlessness for God will give way to perfect and perpetual satisfaction in God.

- Our restlessness for God's word will give way to a beatific vision that renders the Bible no longer necessary.

- Our restlessness for God's salvation will give way to glorified liberation from sin in Christ.

- Our restlessness for God's house will give way to basking continuously in God's holy presence.

- Our restlessness for God's restoration will give way to hearts that lose the ability to wander or leave the God they love.

- Our restlessness for God's mission will give way to a new heaven and a new earth wherein every inhabitant affectionately exalts God with the whole of their humanity.

In between the already of Christ's inaugurated kingdom and the not yet of Christ's consummated kingdom, we are restless. But the consummation will put our restlessness to rest. That is precisely why God's suffering people continually cry, "Come, Lord Jesus!" (Rev. 22:20).

Dangers to Avoid

Thomas Edison failed innumerable times before he designed a filament bulb that was durable and economical. Some say he succeeded after 1,000 failed attempts, while others put the number of disappointments as high as 6,635 or 10,000. Only God really knows! But however you interpret the historical data, there is no question that Edison had a dogged perseverance that would not rest until progress was realized. His unremitting restlessness was the precondition of his success, and it is what carried him through failure after failure.

The ordinary rural farmer in the late nineteenth century was quite content with a kerosene lamp and a candle, but God endowed a man with common-grace restlessness that resulted in technological progress and blessing. Affordable and dependable electric light is an amazing gift that sinners like us don't deserve any more than we deserve the light of the sun! But such innovative blessing would never have been ours if there had not been a discontented man who had a vision for better things to come.

My ambition in this little exposition of the Psalms has not been to expand your theological knowledge or your practical activity. My simple goal has been to expand the vision of your soul. Like Edison, I would never have dreamed of subjecting myself to the painful, frustrating toil of writing had I not been driven with a restless desire to help you to see that there is more of God to be had than you currently possess. With all due respect to candles, *Restless Devotion* is my attempt to snap our little candlesticks so that we might link arms in the restless pursuit of our unsearchable, brilliant God.

There are, however, other ways you could respond to the call of this book. One is with self-exalting legalism, while the other is with self-excusing laxity.

Self-Exalting Legalism

Restlessness can easily become a new form of legalism. We can depend on ourselves in the pursuit of restlessness. Fixating on our doing, our fasting, our praying, our meditating, and our worshiping, we lose sight of the God who alone can awaken true spiritual appetite in us. When the means of grace become ends in themselves, we have fallen into idolatry. When we trust in our own strength to cultivate spiritual hunger, we end up cultivating a spirit of haughtiness.

Such a legalistic heart not only will cause us to depend on self to pursue restlessness but also to depend on restlessness to pursue blessedness. Instead of our hunger provoking us to greater faith in the blessed God, our hunger can subtly become the object of our faith. We come to believe that if we can have just enough earnest desire for God, then He will be duty bound to bless us. Is this not what fuels modern-day revivalism after the order of Charles Finney? His followers think, "We can put revival on the calendar because if we are earnest enough, then

God is duty bound to show up!" But God is not our puppet. He is the Lord, and our restlessness does not back Him into a corner so that He has no choice but to bless. His blessing is free, and it is purely of His grace that He rewards diligent, hungry seekers after Him (Heb. 11:6).

Self-exalting legalism will cause us to compare ourselves to fellow believers, taking pride that we appear more spiritually hungry than they do. A biography I'm reading of George Whitefield, who possessed such a restlessness for God, has tempted me to beat myself up because my hunger for God doesn't drive me to pray through the night and to tirelessly evangelize like he did. The moment we begin to play the comparison game is the moment our restlessness has ceased to be Godward. This is not a competition, nor is it a reason for pride, for whatever genuine desires we have for God are all of His grace! If someone is hungrier than you, be thankful for God's grace in their life and be encouraged to press on. If someone is less hungry than you, be thankful for God's grace in your life and be an encouragement to them to press on.

Self-Excusing Laxity

The other potential response to this book, which is no less arrogant than legalism, is to excuse ourselves. It is really a form of antinomianism that says the spirituality of the Psalter is reserved for super Christians like George Whitefield. Maybe your pastor would profit from a book like this, but for an ordinary layperson like you, it seems a bit over the top.

God gifted us with the Psalter as a songbook and a prayer book so that our souls may be molded according to the spirituality manifested in these inspired utterances, a spirituality that was perfectly realized in the Christ we have been recreated to image. Think of all He has given you in our consideration of the Psalms in this book:

- He gave you Psalm 63 so that you may learn to desire Him.

- He gave you Psalm 119 so that you may cultivate a hunger for His word and make it your day-and-night feast.

- He gave you Psalm 51 so that you may learn to hanker after Christ and all of His saving benefits.

- He gave you Psalm 84 in order to train your soul to restlessly seek His house like you seek no other place.

- He gave you Psalm 126 to stir up discontented desires for the restorative streams of His Spirit.

- He gave you Psalm 67 to transform your vision of the world, that you may burn with a passion for every person to worship God.

- He gave you Psalm 17 to emblazon on your soul the eternal hope that is yours in Christ, that you may look with longing to a resurrected world wherein God's glory is all.

These are not songs for super Christians. They are songs for every Christian. They are songs for *you* that give you a sense of the Godward discontent He desires to stir up in you throughout this wilderness pilgrimage.

Jesus hates spiritual complacency. In the first century, a church had been planted in the town of Laodicea. The town lacked its own water supply, depending on an aqueduct to carry water from a neighboring hot spring. By the time the water reached Laodicea, it was lukewarm. Hot water makes for a refreshing bath and cold water makes for a refreshing drink, but lukewarm water is most undesirable. This church that had experienced God's gospel blessing had become just like its water supply. The risen Lord comes to them with a rebuke, "I know your works, that you are neither cold nor hot. I could wish you were cold or hot" (Rev. 3:15). He then warns the church because of their tepid apathy, "Because you are lukewarm, and neither cold nor hot, I will vomit you out of My mouth" (v. 16). Like a man might spit out lukewarm water in disgust, so Christ is saying He will do the same with this complacent church. Do you see the urgency here? You and I cannot fall prey to self-excusing laxity. If there is complacency in our souls, we must heed Christ's command: "Be zealous and repent" (v. 19). Earnest repentance for our tepid spirituality is the great need because repentance always turns us to the God of grace.

Practically Cultivating Godward Discontent

While we mustn't depend on ourselves in the cultivation of dissatisfied devotion, strenuous action and effort on our part are required. We can't sit on our hands and hope God shows up. We must seek after God, and we must seek after the cultivation of appetite for God. If you find that your soul is not hungry, may I suggest doing a few simple things?

First, commit one of these inspired songs to memory. Hiding it in your heart, meditate on it as you are driving to work, waiting in the checkout line, and lying in bed at night. Mull over the various words and phrases. Make applications to your own heart and life. Seek to get these restless psalms into your spiritual bloodstream.

Second, pray these inspired songs back to God. Make the restless utterances of the psalmist your own, and ask God to work such a holy desire for Him and all things related to Him. The appendix provides you with ideas of how to do this with each of the psalms discussed in this book.

Third, make use of the grace of fasting (assuming you have a green light from your medical physician). Sincere fasting that looks to Christ and depends on His Spirit is a marvelous way not only to communicate hunger for God but also to cultivate it. If you have never fasted before, start small with a twenty-four-hour fast. You presumably fast through the night already, which is why the first meal of the day is called *breakfast* (you are breaking your fast), so if you eat an early dinner and then begin a twenty-four-hour fast, you will be skipping only breakfast and lunch the next day. That being said, it will probably not be easy the first time. One of the reasons people often flounder in fasting is that they don't have a clearly defined purpose for doing it. In this case, your purpose would be to cultivate a personal hunger for God. Keep that purpose before you, and use the time when you would normally eat to seek God in prayer.

Fourth, be present and engaged whenever the doors of your church are opened, especially when God's word is being preached and the sacraments are being administered. It is through His audible and visible word in the midst of His gathered people that God most delights to display His gospel glory, and if you taste and see His goodness, it will make you hanker after more.

Anything that engages your soul with God, His word, His salvation, His house, His restoration, His mission, and His vindication can and ought to be a means of cultivating spiritual appetite. For the Christian, who reads nature through the lens of Scripture, that includes the earth with its multiplicity of beautiful sights, delicious tastes, and exquisite smells—all of which are displaying the glory of the triune God. For me, sometimes the most soul-enlarging exercise is going on a trail run to commune with God as I marvel at His beauty in the mountains, waterfalls, and trees. If all things are from Him and through Him, then shouldn't all things be leading us to Him with a desire to know Him more and to serve Him better?

God-Exalting Discontentment
In the introduction I altered Edison's sage statement, writing, "Show me a thoroughly satisfied Christian, and I will show you a spiritual failure." I hope you are more convinced of that now than when you read it in the opening pages. In this interim between the already and the not yet, there is reason to groan. We have not arrived, and we will not arrive until the consummation. (Even the intermediate state is one of restless longing for resurrection finality.)

There are few satanic threats more subtle and dangerous than spiritual complacency (Amos 6:1), for it makes us settle for a shallow and surface-level spirituality, and it leads us into spiritual declension and covenant-breaking devastation.

The only way to not fall prey to the covenant-breaking cycle set forth in Judges and in all of old covenant history is to press on in our seeing, savoring, and serving the God of grace. We don't have to succumb to spiritual decline in this wilderness world. Discontented desire after God, His word, His salvation, His house, His restoration, His mission, and His vindication can usher us into an ever-expanding cycle of spiritual progress as we learn to pray with increasing wilderness conviction,

> Whom have I in heaven but You?
> And there is none upon earth that I desire
>   besides You.
> My flesh and my heart fail;
> But God is the strength of my heart and my
>   portion forever. (Ps. 73:25–26)

Praying the Psalms

Each of us learns how to pray by listening to others pray. Whether hearing the prayers of a parent, friend, or pastor, we intuitively mimic the language, content, tone, and emotion of the prayers of others for good or for ill.

When it comes to learning how to pray, there are no better prayers to listen to and mimic than the inspired prayers of Scripture. Before many of the psalms were ever sung, they were first prayed. God has given us the Psalter as a prayer book in order to teach us the language, content, tone, and emotion of prayer that brings delight to Him.

True prayer is the heartfelt expression of Godward delight and dependence, which is precisely what we find in every one of the psalms. We ought to shape our prayers accordingly. In saying that, I'm not suggesting that we recite psalms word for word back to God. Instead, I'm suggesting that we root the psalms deep into our hearts so that they naturally (or supernaturally) begin to structure, direct, and infuse our prayers with our unique personalities and in our specific circumstances.

Below you will find general examples of what this might look like, following the ACTS (adoration, confession, thanksgiving, and supplication) prayer model. Nearly every line of the Psalter can be translated into adoration, confession, thanksgiving, and supplication, and I attempt to show you how with each of the psalms expounded and applied in *Restless Devotion*. These are merely ideas to help you to begin to think of the manifold ways God's word can be prayed back to Him. I do not share them in order that you slavishly follow them, nor do I encourage you to slavishly follow ACTS. Many psalms begin with petitions (there is nothing unholy about that), and some psalms don't include petitions at all. ACTS is merely a helpful way to remember the various ways in which we can express our Godward delight and dependence.

I pray this appendix will assist you in molding your prayer life after the restless songs of the Spirit-inspired psalmist.

Praying Psalm 63

Read Psalm 63:1

- Adore God as the ultimate source of soul satisfaction.

- Confess seeking soul satisfaction in the wilderness of this world.

- Thank God that He is *your* God and has taken you to be *His* possession.

- Supplicate God to make you thirst for Him like the psalmist does.

Read Psalm 63:2

- Adore God as the one to whom belongs all power and glory.

- Confess the dimness and smallness of your vision of God.

- Thank God that He savingly dwells in His new covenant temple.
- Supplicate God to enable you and your church to behold Him afresh through His word this coming Lord's Day.

Read Psalm 63:3–4

- Adore God for the astounding reality that He would set His love on a sinner like you.
- Confess how little we relish the love of God in Christ toward us.
- Thank God that His love is better than anything this barren world can offer.
- Supplicate God to shed His love abroad in your heart as the fuel of your praise to Him.

Read Psalm 63:5–7

- Adore God for the saving refuge you have found under His wings.
- Confess unbelief that God will truly satisfy.
- Thank God for His promise to reward those who diligently seek Him.
- Supplicate God to satisfy the members of your church with Himself, causing them to long for Him even more.

Read Psalm 63:8

- Adore God as the one on whom you are entirely dependent for all things pertaining to life and godliness.
- Confess the looseness and weakness of your clinging to God.

- Thank God for specific ways He has upheld you in past days and weeks.
- Supplicate God for specific needs, asking Him to uphold and deliver you by His right hand.

Read Psalm 63:9–11

- Adore God as the defender of His people in this hostile world.
- Confess the fear of the future as the world rages against Christ and His church.
- Thank God for His sure promise that the gates of hell will not prevail against His people.
- Supplicate God to embolden your brothers and sisters who are persecuted for the faith, enabling them to exult in Christ and hope in Christ's future triumph.

Praying Psalm 119

Read Psalm 119:14, 24, 72, 103

- Adore God as a speaking God who has graciously chosen to reveal Himself in the Bible.
- Confess a failure to treasure the Bible as it ought to be treasured.
- Thank God for giving you access to His word in your own language.
- Supplicate God to make your church delight in the sweetness of the Bible.

Read Psalm 119:20, 36, 40, 131

- Adore God for His all-desirable beauty displayed in the Bible.

- Confess being a stranger to this all-consuming longing for God's word.

- Thank God for the gracious inclinations toward the Bible that He works in you.

- Supplicate God that He would give you life in His word, making you long for it more.

Read Psalm 119:11, 15, 16, 97

- Adore God for His loveliness, which makes His word lovely.

- Confess forgetting God's word in times of trial and temptation.

- Thank God for the way His truth sanctifies and keeps you from sin.

- Supplicate God to teach you how to meditate on the Scriptures continuously.

Read Psalm 119:12, 18, 19

- Adore the Holy Spirit as the great opener of spiritual eyes in both regeneration and sanctification.

- Confess reading and hearing God's Word without being prayerfully dependent on God to illumine your mind and heart.

- Thank God for graciously teaching you throughout this earthly pilgrimage.

- Supplicate God to open His word to you, your family, and your church.

Read Psalm 119:28, 67, 71, 92

- Adore God as the Father of mercies who comforts you in your afflictions by His word.

- Confess not looking to the Bible in trials but instead looking elsewhere for comfort and strength.
- Thank God for the way He has used trials to open His word to you and to bring you into greater submission to it.
- Supplicate God to use the Scriptures to strengthen fellow Christians who are undergoing particularly difficult trials.

Read Psalm 119:5, 32, 44, 101

- Adore Christ for His perfect obedience to God's word and for His perfect satisfaction of the penalty for your disobedience to it.
- Confess allowing your feet to run in evil ways in the past week.
- Thank God for delivering you from your bondage to sin and giving you holy desires to obey Him.
- Supplicate God to enlarge your heart that you may run steadfastly in the path of His word.

Read Psalm 119:46, 136, 139

- Adore God for His authority and power over even the kings of the earth.
- Confess a lack of boldness in speaking God's word to the world.
- Thank Christ for His tears for you in your foolish rejection of the truth.
- Supplicate God for your community, nation, and world that He would bring many to believe and love His word.

Praying Psalm 51

Read Psalm 51:1–2

- Adore God for His abundant mercy and covenant love.

- Confess your inability to cleanse yourself from the stain of your sin.
- Thank God that His mercy, grace, and love have reached to you, saving you in your sin and misery.
- Supplicate God to work genuine repentance in your heart so that you go to Him with your sin instead of hiding it from Him.

Read Psalm 51:3–6

- Adore God for His omnipresence and all-seeing eye.
- Confess your woeful condition in Adam, even from conception, and the continual corruption that clings to your soul even in Christ.
- Thank God for teaching you wisdom and truth in Christ so that you may be the object of His delight.
- Supplicate God for greater brokenness over sin as you grasp the sinfulness of sin in the light of His greatness and goodness.

Read Psalm 51:7–9

- Adore God, who is both just and the justifier of those who put their faith in Jesus.
- Confess the infinite guilt of your sin and your inability to pay the debt.
- Thank Christ for being cursed in your place so that you may rejoice.
- Supplicate God for fresh pardon and cleansing from sin in Christ.

Read Psalm 51:10–12

- Adore the Spirit for His thrice holy majesty.

- Confess your need for God to continually renew and uphold you by His grace.
- Thank God that He does not cast off His children, though He may withdraw His felt presence and love.
- Supplicate God for a hatred of all that would grieve or quench the Spirit within so that you may be filled with all of His fullness.

Read Psalm 51:13

- Adore God as a missionary God who sought you when you did not seek Him.
- Confess your failure to share God's gospel with your unbelieving neighbors.
- Thank God for the person(s) He used to teach you about Christ's pardon and power for sinners.
- Supplicate God for a joy in the gospel that would compel you to share it with others.

Read Psalm 51:14–17

- Adore God as your deliverer and Savior.
- Confess the coldness and heartlessness that often mark your public sacrifices of praise.
- Thank God for convicting you of sin so you may have the contrite heart that alone is befitting His worship.
- Supplicate God to cause the gospel of Christ to dwell so richly in your local congregation that the lips of God's people erupt with praise.

Read Psalm 51:18–19

- Adore God for the pleasure He has in prospering His people.

- Confess your great need for God's reviving work.
- Thank God for the ways He has revived your soul and the souls of His people in the past.
- Supplicate God for your congregation and denomination, as well as the faithful churches in your city, nation, and world, that God would do them good.

Praying Psalm 84

Read Psalm 84:1–2

- Adore God as the Lord of Hosts who has life in Himself.
- Confess a lack of desire for His house.
- Thank God for coming down to dwell with creatures and sinners like us.
- Supplicate God for a greater desire for Him that would lead to a greater desire for the place where His glory dwells.

Read Psalm 84:3–4

- Adore God as the one who welcomes all into His house, even the least.
- Confess not grasping the immense privilege of being with God's gathered people in His special presence.
- Thank God for not turning away any from His altars.
- Supplicate God to gather, rule over, and bless your church on this coming Lord's Day.

Read Psalm 84:5–7

- Adore God as the source of your strength.
- Confess looking for strength and refreshment in places other than in God and His gracious ordinances.

- Thank God for the way He refreshes and renews His people through the preached word and sacrament.
- Supplicate God for fellow believers who are weary in their wilderness pilgrimage and in need of His strengthening grace.

Read Psalm 84:8–9

- Adore God as the hearer and answerer of prayer.
- Confess often not seeking God in prayer for His blessing on our corporate worship.
- Thank God for uniting you to His anointed King, Jesus Christ.
- Supplicate God to teach us how to pray and to not allow us to be content with reciting prayers that don't actually reach His ears or receive His answer.

Read Psalm 84:10

- Adore God as the altogether lovely one whose presence is more desirable than anything on this earth.
- Confess pridefully yearning for positions of prominence in the church.
- Thank God for the immense privilege of serving and worshiping in His house.
- Supplicate God to work love for His house in the hearts of members of your congregation who display indifference toward public worship.

Read Psalm 84:11–12

- Adore God as your sun and shield who blesses and protects you.
- Confess questioning God's goodness in this wilderness.

- Thank God for working all things for your good in His love and favor.
- Supplicate God to shield you from all the fiery darts of the Evil One.

Praying Psalm 126

Read Psalm 126:1–2

- Adore God as the gracious reviver and restorer of His people in days gone by.
- Confess forgetting God's past deliverances in your life and in the life of the church.
- Thank God for the way He has visited His people with Spirit-wrought revival in the past.
- Supplicate God to use His mighty working in history past to produce within you a longing for His mighty working in your day.

Read Psalm 126:3

- Adore God for His greatness and the great things He has done for His people in Christ.
- Confess a lack of gladness in God and His reviving grace.
- Thank God for the specific great things He has done for which you are glad.
- Supplicate God to make your church one of glad worship flowing from God's gracious deliverance.

Read Psalm 126:4

- Adore the Holy Spirit for the streams of refreshing grace He infuses into the life of the church.
- Confess that the church today is not all that different

from postexilic Israel, being prone to formalism, luke-warmness, and worldliness.

- Thank God for pouring out His Spirit at Pentecost and for pouring out His Spirit on you in regeneration.

- Supplicate God for revival in your church, your city, your denomination, and your nation.

Read Psalm 126:5–6

- Adore Jesus as the ultimate reaper, who in joy and triumph will gather in His wheat at the end of the age.

- Confess a lack of holy desire, which is evidenced by our lack of tears.

- Thank God for hearing the agonizing cries of His people.

- Supplicate God to teach you what it means to sow with tears—that He would birth within you longing for His power and glory that would move you to groan and cry out to Him.

Praying Psalm 67

Read Psalm 67:1–2

- Adore God for His beauty as it shines on His people in the face of Jesus Christ in the gospel.

- Confess the need for His reviving work individually and corporately.

- Thank God that He does not deal with you as your sins deserve but shows grace even when you wander and grow cold.

- Supplicate God to revive your church so that you would grow in zeal for and engagement in Christ's mission.

Psalm 67:3–5

- Adore God, who alone is worthy of worship.
- Confess a lack of holy passion for the spread of God's worship in the world.
- Thank God for the gladness He has worked in us through His saving gospel.
- Supplicate God for your nation, that He would draw multitudes to Himself, build His church, and establish His praise.

Read Psalm 67:6–7

- Adore God as the sovereign Lord whose purposes for this earth will not fail.
- Confess depending on your own strength and resources to bring about gospel increase.
- Thank God for the incomprehensible grace He displays toward the godless nations.
- Supplicate God that His name would be hallowed among every nation, tribe, and tongue.

Praying Psalm 17

Read Psalm 17:1–5

- Adore God as the just judge who vindicates His people.
- Confess how prosperity and a lack of affliction can lead you to grow prayerless and self-sufficient.
- Thank God for His grace and power in the gospel, which alone can cleanse the conscience and enable us to walk in obedience.
- Supplicate God to vindicate His suffering people around the world.

Read Psalm 17:6–12

- Adore God as our saving refuge who is able to hide His people from the most intense opposition.

- Confess your tendency to take refuge in the things of creation when facing opposition instead of looking to God as deliverer.

- Thank God for making His people the apple (i.e., pupil) of His eye and that you are never outside of His loving, fatherly sight.

- Supplicate God to help your persecuted brothers and sisters to remember God's faithfulness toward His suffering people throughout redemptive history.

Read Psalm 17:13–15

- Adore God as the divine warrior who will strike down His enemies.

- Confess an unbelieving aversion to God's wrath and vengeance.

- Thank God for the unshakable hope we have of resurrection glory in Christ.

- Supplicate God to help His wilderness church store up treasure in heaven and fix their minds on the things above where Christ is.